THE HYPOCRITE

Richard Bean

THE HYPOCRITE

OBERON BOOKS
LONDON

WWW.OBERONBOOKS.COM

First published in 2017 by Oberon Books Ltd
521 Caledonian Road, London N7 9RH
Tel: +44 (0) 20 7607 3637 / Fax: +44 (0) 20 7607 3629
e-mail: info@oberonbooks.com
www.oberonbooks.com

Lyrics on pages 11-12, 27-28, 40-41, 60-61, 89-90, 109 and 122 are
written by Grant Olding, and are reproduced by permission of
Air-Edel Associates Ltd., 18 Rodmarton Street, London W1U 8BJ.

A catalogue record for this book is available from the British
Library.

PB ISBN: 9781786820839
E ISBN: 9781786820846

Cover design © Hull Truck/RSC

Visit www.oberonbooks.com to read more about all our books
and to buy them. You will also find features, author interviews and
news of any author events, and you can sign up for e-newsletters
so that you're always first to hear about our new releases.

RSC
ROYAL
SHAKESPEARE
COMPANY

THE ROYAL SHAKESPEARE COMPANY

The Royal Shakespeare Company creates theatre at its best, made in Stratford-upon-Avon and shared around the world. We produce an inspirational artistic programme each year, setting Shakespeare in context, alongside the work of his contemporaries and today's writers.

Everyone at the RSC – from actors to armourers, musicians to technicians – plays a part in creating the world you see on stage. All our productions begin life at our Stratford workshops and theatres and we bring them to the widest possible audience through our touring, residencies, live broadcasts and online activity. So wherever you experience the RSC, you experience work made in Shakespeare's home town.

We have trained generations of the very best theatre-makers and we continue to nurture the talent of the future. We encourage everyone to enjoy a lifelong relationship with Shakespeare and live theatre. We reach 530,000 children and young people annually through our education work, transforming their experiences in the classroom, in performance and online.

NEW WORK AT THE RSC

Through an extensive programme of research and development, we resource writers, directors and actors to explore and develop new ideas for our stages, and as part of this we commission playwrights to engage with the muscularity and ambition of the classics and to set Shakespeare's world in the context of our own.

We invite writers to spend time with us in our rehearsal rooms, with our actors and creative teams. Alongside developing new plays for all our stages, we invite playwrights to contribute dramaturgically to both our productions of Shakespeare and his contemporaries, as well as our work for, and with, young people. We believe that engaging with living writers and contemporary theatre-makers helps to establish a creative culture within the Company which both inspires new work and creates an ever more urgent sense of enquiry into the classics.

Shakespeare was a great innovator and breaker of rules, as well as a bold commentator on the times in which he lived. It is his spirit which informs new work at the RSC. Erica Whyman, Deputy Artistic Director, heads up this strand of the Company's work alongside Pippa Hill as Literary Manager.

The RSC Acting Companies are generously supported by
THE GATSBY CHARITABLE FOUNDATION and THE KOVNER FOUNDATION.

The work of the RSC Literary Department is generously supported by
THE DRUE HEINZ TRUST.

The RSC is grateful for the significant support of its principal funder, Arts Council England, without which our work would not be possible. Around 75 per cent of the RSC's income is self-generated from Box Office sales, sponsorship, donations, enterprise and partnerships with other organisations.

Supported using public funding by
**ARTS COUNCIL
ENGLAND**

HULL TRUCK THEATRE

Hull Truck Theatre tells powerful human stories that resonate with our times.

We have been creating exciting performances for over 45 years, starting with a group of friends making theatre in the back of a truck, to a venue on Spring Street, to our purpose-built home on Ferensway.

The company began in 1972 after director Mike Bradwell placed a magazine advert reading 'half-formed theatre company seeks other half'. Various artists responded, moved to Hull and began devising their own plays — Hull Truck Theatre was born. An anarchic spirit and a passion for telling stories were at the heart of the company from the very beginning and brought our performances to national attention.

In the 1980s John Godber took the helm. We moved to our first permanent building, a renovated church hall on Hull's Spring Street, creating a stream of popular hits which toured to great acclaim.

In 2012 we celebrated our 40th anniversary by moving into a new home on Ferensway, and the following year Artistic Director Mark Babych joined to lead the company on the next stage of our journey.

We create exceptional drama which builds on traditions laid down by writers including Anthony Minghella and Alan Plater, as well as creating new work with artists such as Tom Wells, Tanika Gupta and Bryony Lavery. We make work with local people, programme the very best in live performance and build partnerships with others to create a vibrant and dynamic cultural hub for Hull that is inspiring, creative and welcoming.

Hull Truck Theatre gratefully acknowledges support from:

Supported using public funding by
ARTS COUNCIL ENGLAND

Hull City Council

HULL UK CITY OF CULTURE 2017

The story so far...

When in 2013 it was announced that Hull was to be UK City of Culture 2017, the city erupted with huge excitement.

It's an award given every four years to a city that demonstrates the belief in the transformative power of culture. Here was an unprecedented opportunity to put Hull on the map and to help build a legacy, positioning it as a place to live, visit, study and invest in.

Culture Company (Hull 2017), established to deliver on that promise, set out to produce 365 days of great art and cultural events inspired by the city and told to the world. The ambition was to create a nationally significant event that celebrates the unique character of Hull, its people and heritage. It offers a programme that takes in every art form, from theatre and performance, to visual arts and literature, to music and film, which goes into every corner of the city, whilst showcasing it nationally.

Working with local as well as national and international artists and cultural institutions, Hull 2017 also draws on the distinctive spirit of the city and the artists, writers, directors, musicians, revolutionaries and thinkers that have made such a significant contribution to the development of art and ideas.

The positive reaction to the programme has exceeded all expectations, with Hull now being taken seriously as a cultural destination for must-see events. This includes the sell-out *The Hypocrite*, the first of a jam-packed theatre programme for 2017, which has been curated to challenge and thrill new and existing audiences in the city and beyond.

The Hypocrite was co-produced by the Royal Shakespeare Company, Hull Truck Theatre and Hull UK City of Culture 2017. It was first performed at Hull Truck Theatre on 24 February 2017. The production transferred to the Swan Theatre, Stratford-upon-Avon on 31 March 2017.

SIR JOHN HOTHAM	**Mark Addy**
LORD MAYOR BARNARD	**Martin Barrass**
DRUDGE	**Danielle Bird**
MESSENGER/SOLDIER/LOCAL	**Rachel Dale**
PEREGRINE PELHAM	**Neil D'Souza**
CONNIE	**Laura Elsworthy**
KING CHARLES I/GHOST	**Ben Goffe**
SWEET LIPS/MME FROTTAGE/ LADY DIGBY	**Danielle Henry**
EXECUTIONER/CAPTAIN MOYER	**Adrian Hood**
CAPTAIN JACK	**Asif Khan**
PETERS/MESSENGER/SOLDIER	**Andrew Langtree**
JAMES, DUKE OF YORK	**Jordan Metcalfe**
FRANCES HOTHAM	**Sarah Middleton**
DURAND HOTHAM	**Pierro Niel-Mee**
PRINCE RUPERT OF THE RHEIN	**Rowan Polonski**
ALBERT CALVERT	**Paul Popplewell**
LADY SARAH HOTHAM née ANLABY	**Caroline Quentin**
THE RANTER	**Josh Sneesby**
JOHN SALTMARSH	**Matt Sutton**

All other parts played by members of the Company.

The Hypocrite is a recipient of an EDGERTON FOUNDATION NEW PLAYS AWARD.

Director	**Phillip Breen**
Designer	**Max Jones**
Lighting Designer	**Tina MacHugh**
Music and Lyrics	**Grant Olding**
Sound Designer	**Andrea J Cox**
Stunts and Movement	**Annie Lees-Jones**
Fight Director	**Renny Krupinski**
Illusionist	**Chris Fisher**
Text and Voice Work	**Michaela Kennen**
Assistant Director	**Becky Hope-Palmer**
Music Director	**Phill Ward**
RSC Casting Directors	**Helena Palmer** **Matthew Dewsbury**
Dramaturg	**Pippa Hill**
Production Manager	**Jacqui Leigh**
Transfer Production Manager	**Carl Root**
Costume Supervisor	**Sian Thomas**
Props Supervisor	**Beckie May**
Company Stage Manager	**Paul Sawtell**
Deputy Stage Manager	**Bryony Rutter**
Assistant Stage Manager	**Amy Hawthorne**
Rehearsal Musical Director	**Paul Frankish**
Hull Truck Theatre Producer	**Rowan Rutter**
RSC Producer	**Kevin Fitzmaurice**

MUSICIANS

Music performed live by

Guitar/mandolin/percussion/voice	**Phill Ward**
Double Bass	**Adam Jarvis**

This text may differ slightly from the play as performed.

LOVE THE RSC?

Become a Member or Patron and support our work

The RSC is a registered charity. Our aim is to stage theatre at its best, made in Stratford-upon-Avon and shared around the world with the widest possible audience and we need your support.

Become an RSC Member from £50 per year and access up to three weeks of Priority Booking, advance information, exclusive discounts and special offers, including free on-the-day seat upgrades.

Or support as a Patron from £150 per year for up to one additional week of Priority Booking, plus enjoy opportunities to discover more through special behind-the-scenes events.

For more information visit **www.rsc.org.uk/support** or call the RSC Membership Office on 01789 403440.

THE ROYAL SHAKESPEARE COMPANY

HULL TRUCK THEATRE

Hull Truck Theatre is a creative community of people dedicated to delivering exceptional theatre for a diverse audience, including those encountering it for the first time.

As part of our Hull UK City of Culture 2017 programme we're producing work at an unprecedented scale with some of the largest cast sizes ever to grace our stages.

We are thrilled to be working with an exceptional range of internationally renowned artists and companies, commissioning writers to produce world premières right here in Hull and working with local people to tell their own unique stories.

We see culture as a powerful regenerative tool for our city, enabling it to meet its ambitions and commitment to overcoming social and economic challenges. We are a pioneering theatre with a unique Northern Voice, locally rooted, global in outlook, inspiring artists, audiences and communities to reach their greatest potential.

Through our work with schools and with the community, we help to raise aspirations and give life-changing creative opportunities to thousands of young people, disabled groups and adults.

'We believe that everyone has the right to enjoy and be enriched by high quality artistic work that is culturally relevant to people and place, in a positive and welcoming environment. We aim to be a thriving creative organisation that tells extraordinary human stories, offering fresh and imaginative perspectives on the world.'

Mark Babych, Artistic Director

ACKNOWLEDGEMENTS

I'd like to thank Panda Cox, Ron Fairfax, Dr Andrew Hopper and Hull History Centre for helping with the research.

The idea of the play was welcomed by Greg Doran of the RSC, and we should all be grateful when doors open, instead of being slammed in our faces.

The development of the script was not my task alone, and I'd like to thank Pippa Hill of the RSC Literary Team, Mark Babych of Hull Truck, Phil Breen, Erica Whyman, Chris Campbell and the actors for their insight and contributions.

An army marches on its stomach, so we must credit Ally and Jo in the Adelaide Street chip shop for a continuous supply of haddock and chips and mushy peas.

Characters

SIR JOHN HOTHAM

LADY SARAH HOTHAM

DURAND HOTHAM

FRANCES HOTHAM

CAPTAIN JACK HOTHAM

CONNIE

CAPTAIN MOYER

SWEET LIPS

MADEMOISELLE FROTTAGE

LADY DIGBY

JOHN SALTMARSH

LORD MAYOR BARNARD

ALBERT CALVERT

PEREGRINE PELHAM (MEMBER FOR HULL)

DUKE OF YORK

PRINCE RUPERT

KING CHARLES

THE GHOST OF MARY ASCOUGH

THE RANTER

MR. PETERS (OFFICER OF EXECUTIONS)

THE COMPANY TO PLAY – SOLDIERS, MESSENGERS, WHORES,
THE MOB, MEMBERS OF THE FAMILY OF LOVE, ALDERMEN,
LONDONERS ETC

SET

An open stage that can become indoor rooms,
and outdoor street scenes, both London, and Hull.

PROLOGUE

London 1645. Before the Tower of London. An execution block and basket on a plinth. The mob mill and wait for the execution. Costermongers, cutpurses, beggars, soldiers. Chuggers try to collect money and signatures for the Ranters, Seekers, Anabaptists, Familists, Levellers, Diggers from the audience. Each actor is knowledgeable about their movement and has pamphlets. Entrepreneurs try and sell souvenir block and axe carvings.

Enter CONNIE, speaking with a Hull accent.

CONNIE: *In a world turned upside down*
Our story starts at the end
The epilogue, usurps the prologue
And is by a woman penned

COSTERMONGER 1: Thames oysters! Surprise the wife!

COSTERMONGER 2: Sea coals!? Come on muvver sort it out!

> *CONNIE passes a chugger, with waistcoat, quill and pamphlet, representing the Levellers.*

CHUGGER 1: Good morning ma'am, could you spare a minute for the Levellers –

CONNIE: – sorry luv, I'm late.

Our play begins in London, unfortunately,
A terrible place, unlike mi cultured 'ull.
The English revolution is full blown,
Parliament's king, and the King's annulled

> *An aristocrat fallen on hard times pleads with her.*

LORD BEGGAR: For a lord now emulated. Spare change please?!

CONNIE: I'm from Yorkshire love, we don't have spare change.

Lords beg and the beggars are all on horse,
Charles Stuart slips from shire to fen

> *Like poor Tom, in plays of old,*
> *Searching for a hearth and the hearts of men.*

DRUNKEN RANTER: I, aye me, I am the Lord your God!

CONNIE: *God's a shattered Baptist, Ranter, Quaker,*
> *And if He lives in this new republic*
> *He's in the book, in the stocks, or in His grave*
> *God's now owt you like, 'cept Catholic*

> *A RANTER's CHUGGER approaches CONNIE.*

CHUGGER 2: Spare a couple of minutes for the Diggers?

CONNIE: – I signed up yesterday love!

> *In accord with the discord of the age,*
> *When traditions burn up like parchment in the fire,*
> *We'll begin our comedy at the end,*
> *With the tragic execution of a friend*

> > *Drums. Enter a dwarf executioner with a small axe.*
> > *Followed by a medium executioner with a medium axe,*
> > *then a huge executioner with a huge axe. Then SIR JOHN*
> > *HOTHAM. Also, HUGH PETERS, the executing officer, and*
> > *DURAND HOTHAM. The crowd boo.*

PETERS: Sir John Hotham, Governor of Hull -

MOB: Hypocrite!

MOB: We needed Hull, you damned feculent shit breech!

PETERS: – guilty of betrayal of trust to Parliament and adherence to the King.

MOB: Traitor!

WHORE: You wanna last kiss love?!

MOB: He's a right mutton monger!

PETERS: – guilty, of refusing to supply Lord Fairfax with powder –

MOB 2: – I got snuff! Who wants snuff?!

PETERS: – guilty of intent to betray Hull.

MOB: *(Furious.)* Turncoat / Papist / Renegade / dog!

MOB: Wanker.

PETERS: To the block.

SIR JOHN: May I speak to London?

PETERS: The prisoner is not to speak!

> *HOTHAM is led to the block.*

DURAND: Why shan't my father speak?

PETERS: The prisoner commends to the people his terrestrial life, namely, the mask of honour –

MOB: – Woah!

PETERS: – the emptiness of words

MOB: – Woah!

PETERS: – and the betrayal of friends. All else is vanity!

> *Laughter.*

CONNIE: Lord Fairfax is behind this!

PETERS: Silence! Do the deed.

EXECUTIONER: Come on! Chop, chop!

> *SIR JOHN takes off his coat and gives it to DURAND. The crowd cheer at every offering. He takes off his gloves and gives them to DURAND. He then takes off his wig and gives it to DURAND. He takes out his false/wooden teeth and gives them to DURAND. He then thinks…is that everything…and kneels and places his head on the block. The EXECUTIONER takes a step forward and raises his axe. SIR JOHN raises a hand and sits up, and takes out his glass eye and gives it to DURAND. Big cheer. He places his head back on the block. The EXECUTIONER swings the axe and with one blow SIR JOHN's head is separated from his body. The mob gasp, but are respectfully silent. The executioner picks the head out, shows it to the mob and hands it to DURAND. DURAND puts his*

father's head on his coffin downstage. Silence is broken by a
COSTERMONGER trying to sell his wife.

COSTERMONGER 3: Wife for sale! Two guineas. Always up for
a tumble, good cook, don't talk much. Interested? I think
you are!

PETERS: Next execution, noon tomorrow. Monsieur André
Picq, for papism and being a bit French.

EXECUTIONER: The fun's over! Move on!

The mob disperse. The bloodied, separated head speaks.

SIR JOHN: I am called traitor, changeling, ambidexter, yet
I have been constant to Parliament, and, unfortunately,
also constant to the King. Honour is contained in motive.
I never gave a thought to saving my own skin, or the
fate of my vast estates across Holderness. I will miss East
Yorkshire, most of which I own.

I leave a pack of hounds, a pet snake and seventeen
children. My first wife, Catherine, awaits me in heaven. My
second wife, the fragrant Anne, will be sat beside her. My
third wife, Jane, *(Spits blood.)* is in Hell, probably running
it. My fourth wife, Catherine, whom I married because she
reminded me of my first wife, Catherine, I shall woo again.
My fifth wife, Sarah Anlaby, survives me, and for her, life
will be perilous, but at least she has a road in West Hull
named after her. Connie, my cook –

CONNIE: – I'm here John!

SIR JOHN: – Connie!? I bequeath to you and your like, the
common people, *(Spits.)* a new politic, constitutional
parliamentary democracy.

(To the audience.) And to you, the audience, I give the
torments of my life as light entertainment.

SONG – WORLD TURNED UPSIDE DOWN

THE KING IS NOW A BEGGAR AND THE BEGGAR'S NOW A GOD.
THE BISHOP'S IN THE GUTTER AND HIS STAFF'S A CATTLE PROD.
THE DIGGER WANTS MORE KNOWLEDGE AND THE RANTER
WANTS THE CROWN
THE PEASANT WANTS FOR NOTHING IN A WORLD TURNED UPSIDE
DOWN.

WE'RE LIVING IN A WORLD TURNED UPSIDE DOWN
WE'RE LIVING IN A TIME TURNED INSIDE OUT.
WE'RE LIVING IN A WORLD TURNED UPSIDE DOWN.
HOW DID THIS COME ABOUT?

THE LAYMAN IS THE EXPERT AND THE MANY RULE THE FEW
WE'RE LEVELLING THE LAND TO BUILD OUR ALBION ANEW.
THE SHOOTS OF GREEN WILL SOON EMERGE OUT OF THE FIELDS
OF BROWN
BY STANDING ON YOUR HEAD YOU SEE THE WORLD TURNED
UPSIDE DOWN.

WE'RE LIVING IN A WORLD TURNED UPSIDE DOWN
WE'RE LIVING IN A TIME TURNED INSIDE OUT.
WE'RE LIVING IN A WORLD TURNED UPSIDE DOWN.
HOW DID THIS COME ABOUT?

NO IDOLS FOR TO WORSHIP AND NO ROYALTY TO SERVE,
TO LIVE AND LOVE AS FREEBORN MEN'S NO MORE THAN WE
DESERVE.
THE KING IS NOW A ROVER, AND A KNAVE IS NOW A KING.
THE WORLD TURNED UPSIDE IS SUCH AN EDIFYING THING.

WE'RE LIVING IN A WORLD TURNED UPSIDE DOWN
WE'RE LIVING IN A TIME TURNED INSIDE OUT.
WE'RE LIVING IN A WORLD TURNED UPSIDE DOWN.
HOW DID THIS COME ABOUT?

WE'RE LIVING IN A WORLD TURNED UPSIDE DOWN
WE'RE LIVING IN A TIME TURNED INSIDE OUT.
WE'RE LIVING IN A WORLD TURNED UPSIDE DOWN.
HOW'D IT ALL COME ABOUT?

Act One

Indoors at the Hotham estate just outside Beverley. The servant, DRUDGE
SCULLION is revealed to be hanging from a hook on the fireplace. On
the floor beneath him is the animal head he has replaced. He seems to
be asleep. There is a pool of urine on the boards beneath him. Enter
CONNIE, the cook, a servant.

CONNIE: *That was the end, but where do we begin?*
   Hotham Hall, Beverley, ten mile from Hull, and home of his kin,
   eleven times passed from Hotham father to Hotham son,
   1642, the English Civil War is brewing, but has not begun

   Enter SIR JOHN followed by LADY SARAH.

SARAH: Whose side are we on!?

SIR JOHN: You, as my wife, are on my side!

SARAH: The servants need to know.

SIR JOHN: The servants will be told when I have decided!

SARAH: You'll take the side of Parliament.

SIR JOHN: Will I?

SARAH: Because they have promised to make you commander
   of all Yorkshire.

SIR JOHN: If I decide to affiliate with Parliament it will be a
   decision born of principle and unrelated to the possibility
   of being made commander of all Yorkshire.

SARAH: With a stipend of three thousand a year.

SIR JOHN: I am loyal to the Stuarts –

SARAH: – because they gave you a knighthood!

SIR JOHN: – do you honestly believe that three thousand
   pounds would turn me to Parliament?

SARAH: In our present financial predicament yes, absolutely.

SIR JOHN: Anyway, what's it got to do with you, you overbosomed prune?!

SARAH: Urgh! Why did I marry such a pompous, half-wiped arse!

SIR JOHN: Why did I marry such a prick shrinking, scrotum breathed, dried up vale of nothing!

SARAH: For the two pig farms that made up the dowry!

Enter CONNIE.

SIR JOHN: A marvellous lunch Connie.

SARAH: What name do you give to that heinous crime?

CONNIE: Mutton casserole.

SARAH: The meat was off!

CONNIE: I got it in fresh, for your return from London.

SARAH: I was delayed a week!

CONNIE: Not my fault then is it.

SARAH: Insolence! The air may be thick with revolution but there'll be no innovations in this house.

CONNIE: Are we for Parliament?

SARAH: We've not yet been told.

CONNIE: And what if any of us in service incline to the King?

SIR JOHN: Do you?

CONNIE: Charles is a runt. If he'd been born a pig, he'd be in a pie. But he is God's choice.

SARAH: Sir John will decide and if you don't approve you can hawk your mutton elsewhere.

CONNIE: Aye, I might. My own bakers' shop.

SARAH: It's two shilling to incorporate into the guild, if you're a man. You'd need a thousand pounds to grease their palms.

CONNIE: I'll get mesen a new dream then.

    CONSTANCE leaves.

SARAH: Drudge! *(To SIR JOHN.)* Why did you put Drudge on his hook?

SIR JOHN: To teach him not to be old and incontinent.

    Urine drips out of DRUDGE's trouser bottoms forming a puddle on the floor. SARAH takes a walking stick and whacks him unbelievably hard on a shin. No response and then he slowly opens an eye, and mimes agony.

SARAH: Get down!

DRUDGE: *(Mimes that he can't.)*

    SARAH pulls at DRUDGE's feet and he is slowly pulled out of his clothes until free but in his underwear. His clothes stay on the hook.

SARAH: Go and watch the road.

    DRUDGE exits staggering.

SARAH: And what kind of week have you had?

SIR JOHN: Without you around? A peaceful, productive week, unplagued by thoughts of suicide. You were late.

SARAH: My horse fell lame, near Doncaster. I had to stay at your cousin's.

SIR JOHN: Very convenient.

SARAH: He was generous, in his hospitality.

    Enter SALTMARSH, a louche looking individual. SARAH and he touch, unseen by SIR JOHN.

And he accompanied me on the road.

SIR JOHN: Reverend cousin!? What brings you to East Yorkshire? We have no virgins.

SALTMARSH: I escorted your wife from Doncaster.

SIR JOHN: I am told that she was delayed a week at your house.

SARAH mimes first a horse, and then a lame horse.

SALTMARSH: Yes, her horse… I taught her horse…some dressage.

SIR JOHN: Lame. Her horse fell lame.

SALTMARSH: Yes! A lame horse. No matter, your wife is pleasant company.

SIR JOHN: Is she? I'm surprised you could find the time given the demands of your congregation. How many wives do you have now?

SALTMARSH: The Family of Love continues to flourish.

SIR JOHN: How come everyone else makes do with one wife at a time but you –

SARAH: – Your reverend cousin needs a thousand a year to continue his work with the congregation.

SIR JOHN: I was told Lord Selby has delivered an eviction order on your human menagerie.

SALTMARSH: May 1st.

SIR JOHN: I don't give alms.

He grabs some papers and thrusts them at SALTMARSH.

And I don't believe you've paid your Ship Money.

SALTMARSH: I'll not pay that tax to the King.

SIR JOHN: As Sherriff I am charged by the King to collect.

SALTMARSH: Have you paid your Ship Money?

SARAH: He's not paid.

SIR JOHN: It's a punitive, unjust tax, and I've no intention of paying! But! It is my duty to collect it!

SARAH: John wishes to impress Pym and Parliament by not paying, but maintain good relations with the King by collecting.

SALTMARSH: How can one soul minister to such varied agendas?

25

SIR JOHN: As you satisfy your various wives cus, with sweet words, vigorously, and one at a time. Doncaster's that way!

SALTMARSH leaves.

Lame horse indeed.

Enter FRANCES, reading a book of poetry. She reads in a frenzy of passion.

SARAH: She has discovered Shakespeare.

SIR JOHN: Oh no! Not that acrimonious, wormy, scrote?! Why did you teach her to read?! To what purpose?! A girl?!

SARAH: So that she might read your will to me as I grieve, at leisure, in my bath.

SIR JOHN: I sent you to London to find the damned giglet a rich husband!

She shows him a small framed woodcut of PELHAM.

SARAH: And here he is.

SIR JOHN: He's covered in scars.

SARAH: It's a woodcut.

SIR JOHN: Do I know him?

SARAH: Peregrine Pelham. The Member for Hull.

SIR JOHN: He's a damned Puritan zealot! He won't approve of my billiards, my snuff, my drinking. I'll have to stop shitting off the bridge.

SARAH: We'd all like that.

SIR JOHN: It's my bridge and it's my river!

SARAH: Pelham is favoured by John Pym, the leader of the House!

SIR JOHN: Is he? Excellent. Well done.

SARAH: He's a gold merchant and keeper of running cash.

SIR JOHN: The kind of son-in-law who could mortgage these estates!?

SARAH: Two problems. He is demanding a dowry of two thousand and Frances is refusing.

SIR JOHN: Horses refuse, not daughters! Why is she reluctant?

SARAH: She met him. *(Beat.)* Do we have two thousand?

SIR JOHN: Argh, money, money, money! Ten years of bad harvests and every day I'm working to keep the wolf from the door! One of these days I'm tempted just to let the bastard in!

SARAH: I'll tell him no then.

SIR JOHN: No! We have to mortgage. And I want her out the house. Frances! Your mother has found you a suitable husband.

FRANCES: He may suit you father, but I do not love him.

SIR JOHN: The aristocracy do not marry for love.

SARAH: If it's passion you want, go and kill a fox.

FRANCES: Peregrine Pelham is fifty-six.

SIR JOHN: And he'll be fifty-seven next year so the sooner you marry him the better!

FRANCES: I want a lover who, unaided, can climb the stairs!

SARAH: There are advantages to an elderly husband. Financial security, property, and an early death.

FRANCES: I don't want to die early!

SARAH: *His* early death.

FRANCES: I want to choose, swoon, and be wooed!

SIR JOHN: You want to be wooned, swooed, and chooed do you!?

FRANCES: If I had love I would want for nothing!

SARAH: Have you ever tried living in a hedge?

FRANCES: It would be an abundant, prolific and opulent hedge if it were furnished with love! Every thorn would be a caress and –

SIR JOHN: – if I choose a damned feculent windmill then you will marry a damned feculent windmill!

Enter DURAND.

FRANCES: My brother can marry for love, but not I!

FRANCES bursts into tears.

SIR JOHN: Fall in love?! Him?! There's more chance of me volunteering to cut off the end of my own cock!

DURAND: Love, I'm told, arrives, uninvited, like a storm, everybody gets wet, and then it passes painfully, like a stubborn stool.

SARAH: *(Aside.)* Merton College Oxford.

SIR JOHN: Be warned, that brief, thrilling hurricane can turn into forty years of drizzle.

DURAND: I love what the minds of learned men have distilled into perfection over generations, namely the law.

SIR JOHN: Your sweetheart, the law, will be of no use in this coming conflict.

DURAND: On which side of the dichotomy in the body politic do we fall?

SIR JOHN: Eh?

SARAH: Which of the two sides are we on?!

SIR JOHN: I know what bichotomy means!

SARAH: Then think on, for my life, all our lives depend on your decision.

SARAH leaves.

DURAND: Surely Parliament. You represent Beverley.

SIR JOHN: I didn't lose an eye in the thirty years war fighting for the Stuarts to sign up for the other side in a civil war.

DURAND: You didn't lose an eye *fighting*. It was a drunken, camp fire jape which involved half an ounce of gunpowder and a live hedgehog.

SIR JOHN: In extremis men will always blow up hedgehogs for a laugh. And, the thirty years war did have the odd lull.

DURAND: Has John Pym made you commander of all Yorkshire?

SIR JOHN: Not yet. But who is better qualified?

DURAND: Fairfax.

The hounds bark, go crazy. They wait, reluctantly, resigned.

SIR JOHN: Fairfax is not a Lord!

The hounds bark again.

He…bought a title like I'd buy a kipper

SIR JOHN ends up with his finger stuck in the ink well.

SIR JOHN: Connie! Durand, leave us a moment.

DURAND leaves. CONNIE comforts HOTHAM.

Connie. I need to choose between the King or the House. Between the right and moral thing to do and the expedient, self serving. It's not easy. And I've got my finger stuck in an ink well.

CONNIE: Do what you always do. Convince yourself that the expedient, self-serving path is the right and moral choice.

She spits on a hanky and rubs his finger clean.

SIR JOHN: Brilliant! To be common as muck, like you, must be really awful, but the blessing is you're free and have no responsibilities. Have you bathed?

CONNIE: Not this year.

SIR JOHN: Tonight.

> *She kisses him and turns to leave. Enter DRUDGE followed by a messenger.*

DRUDGE: *(Mimes having found a messenger on the road.)*

SIR JOHN: You found this man on the road, a messenger.

> *Enter FRANCES, she swoons on the sight of a man.*

FRANCES: Oh! A young man!

SIR JOHN: In whose employ do you serve as a messenger?

MESSENGER: *(Utterly unintelligible Irish accent.) I've come two days on foot from the north of the county in the employ there of the Earl of Newcastle as you well know one of the King's loyal men, aye, I have, so, aye.*

SIR JOHN: Are you Irish?

MESSENGER: *(Unintelligible.) County Offally.*

SIR JOHN: Sirrah, speak up, this is an RSC production and there are people here who will write letters if they can't hear you.

> *Enter SARAH.*

SARAH: RSC and Hull Truck co-production.

SIR JOHN: Sorry! Sarah, your mother was Irish.

SARAH: *(Equally unintelligible.) Now come on there young fellah, who sent you, and what's the message or give us a letter. There. So.*

MESSENGER: *(Unintelligible.) The Earl of Newcastle commands you to take Hull and the arsenal for the King.*

SARAH: He's a messenger from the Earl of Newcastle who commands you to take Hull for the King working under Newcastle's authority.

SIR JOHN: Moi? Serve *under*?! Beneath? Au de sous de. The Earl of Newcastle?! He's a poet, and worse still, a playwright. Drudge, bring me my sword!

> *DRUDGE goes off to get a huge sword, which he drags along the floor.*

Sirrah, honour prevents me from serving under a lyricist. And my honour is like a maiden's honesty, not to be repaired, once broken.

FRANCES: I don't understand.

SIR JOHN: My honour is like a maiden's honesty, not to be repaired, once broken.

FRANCES: Her honesty, once broken?

DURAND: *Her honesty* is a euphemism.

FRANCES: For what?

SARAH: Your damned hymen!

FRANCES: *(FRANCES slips into a pleasurable swooning faint.)* Ooooh!

SIR JOHN: Newcastle cannot give law unto those from whom he should be receiving law! Leave, or die!?

> *SIR JOHN lifts the sword with difficulty. The MESSENGER throws down a thousand pounds in coin.*

MESSENGER: *(Unintelligible.)* A thousand pounds, there, you know, aye, so there is.

SARAH: *(Intelligible.)* A thousand pounds, there, you know, aye, so there is.

> *HOTHAM looks at FRANCES.*

FRANCES: No father, it's not enough. Pelham demands two thousand.

> *Silence as HOTHAM thinks.*

HOTHAM: It's half way there. Sirrah, I accept this weighty calling, without hesitation. Go north with news of my willing service, don't falter.

> *The MESSENGER leaves.*

DURAND: Are we now, because of this turn, for the King?

SARAH: John, do not be rash! Today is not a good time to make profound decisions. Mars is in opposition to Venus.

SIR JOHN: Mars? Venus? I'm the member for Beverley!

SARAH: The heavens are in tumult.

SIR JOHN: I've got enough problems without you dragging in the firmament!

> *Enter CAPTAIN JACK at a burst. He's in military uniform with sword. CONNIE trails in his wake.*

SIR JOHN: Jack. My eldest son!

JACK: Father!

> *JACK throws his arms to embrace his father.*

FRANCES: My big half brother by one of my father's earlier wives!

CONNIE: *(Aside.)* Is that all clear?

SARAH: What news from London, Jack?

JACK: London is a dog in the slips! The King launched the first cannonade and Pym, Haslerig, Holles, Hampden, and William Strode are blown away.

SIR JOHN: He's executed five members by cannon fire?!

JACK: No, that was a metaphor.

SIR JOHN: Oh! Can you please not use metaphor Jack, it's too exciting.

SARAH: We weren't there, we just want to know what happened.

JACK: Similes?

SARAH: If you must!

JACK: The King, like Hercules in a bad mood, with troop, entered the House intent on arresting the five but seeing that they were like absent he said "I see the birds have flown".

DURAND: That's a metaphor.

SIR JOHN: Why would he have them arrested?

JACK: He believed the unstoppable tide –

DURAND: – metaphor.

JACK: The King thought the members had colluded with the London mob, encouraging them to rise against him *like* an unstoppable tide.

SIR JOHN: That has been the constant fear of his Queen.

JACK: The Catholic Queen Henrietta is a stoat in the henhouse.

DURAND: No!

JACK: Like a stoat in the like henhouse, in the night, in search of eggs, she has stolen the crown jewels!

ALL: What! / No?! / good Lord!

JACK: The masked stoat Queen, like a masked stoat in like disguise, has fled to Holland intent on selling the eggs –

SIR JOHN: – what eggs?!

DURAND: Metaphor.

SARAH: – the jewels.

JACK: To expedite the raising of ten thousand foot.

FRANCES: What use are ten thousand feet?

DURAND: The metonym, foot, is used to signify an infantryman.

FRANCES: Is ten thousand foot, five thousand soldiers?

SARAH: With two feet each.

DURAND: Ten thousand foot is ten thousand soldiers.

FRANCES: Only if they're one legged.

SIR JOHN: Women!?

SARAH: Jack! You've been to military school. If an enemy has ten thousand foot –

FRANCES: – and all their soldiers had two legs –

33

SARAH: – how many soldiers would you be facing?

JACK: *(Thinks hard.)* Either five or ten thousand.

SIR JOHN: Out! Now! All the women out!

JACK: The King has flown.

DURAND: He can fly can he?

JACK: Like a hawk the King has like flown to York, where he prowls.

DURAND: Hawks don't prowl.

JACK: Like a cat he prowls, ready to swoop like a hawk, on Hull. Cat / hawk / hawk / cat.

SIR JOHN: *(To CONNIE.)* Connie, what is the meaning of this penny theatre?

CONNIE: Whoever secures the arsenal at Hull wins the war.

DURAND: Who have Parliament appointed as commander of all of Yorkshire?

JACK: My father's enemy.

SIR JOHN: Not…?

JACK: Yes. Fairfax.

> *The dogs bark, go crazy. JACK throws his heavy sword to DRUDGE, who catches it, overbalances and falls over.*

JACK: But I have orders for you too father. This letter from Pym commissions you to take Hull, secure the arsenal, and lock out the Royalist wolves, who might devour the munitions like wolves, if wolves liked gunpowder.

FRANCES: Yes! I want to go to Hull! Out here there are no boys or shops!

CAPTAIN JACK: Pym requires you and three hundred horse to take Hull.

FRANCES: *(In a panic.)* How can my father, alone, with only three hundred stupid horses take Hull? Or are they vicious siege attack horses?

DURAND: *Horse* for *horse and rider*, cavalry.

FRANCES: *(Collapses in relief.)* Ooh.

SIR JOHN: But I cannot serve under the self raising Lord Fairfax.

> *The hounds bark, go crazy.*

SARAH: From now on Lord – you know – we call Black Tom.

> *One lone dog barks – the only one that knows he's also called Black Tom.*

CAPTAIN JACK: John Pym is financing you!

> *JACK throws a bag of coins on to the floor.*

SIR JOHN: That poodle can't buy my reputation! I am committed to the King.

CAPTAIN JACK: One thousand for the billeting of the troops.

SIR JOHN: Another thousand?! One thousand plus one thousand, that's...

CONNIE: – Two thousand.

FRANCES: No! No! No!

> *FRANCES runs out.*

SARAH: John, that money is from Parliament to secure Hull.

SIR JOHN: I can't live for one more day with that incessant, febrile inamorata, and we need Pelham to secure the estates.

SARAH: It cannot be used as her dowry!

SIR JOHN: Watch me. Prepare for Hull! Durand! A letter, to John Pym.

DURAND: Dear John.

SIR JOHN: Noble sir, supreme authority of this nation, leader of Parliament, trust that I shall serve you until the death of time, without sway, sans bending, sans – what's another word for bend?

DURAND: Er…stoop, lean, squat.

SIR JOHN: Sans squatting.

DURAND: Unswerving.

SIR JOHN: Good. I accept your commission, and shall tomorrow, for there is no day sooner, secure Hull for Parliament.

SARAH: So we're for Parliament now?

SIR JOHN: We're on both sides you witless sphincter shrinker! Get out! Everybody!

> *CONNIE remains. She knows that "everybody" doesn't include her.*

Sweet chestnut, what have I done?

CONNIE: You have betrayed the King, and betrayed Parliament.

HOTHAM: Yes, it's been a full day.

CONNIE: Best make sure we end up on the winning side.

> *CONNIE leaves.*

END OF SCENE

Act Two

SCENE ONE

Hull, inside the walls. Busy with soldiers, and trained band members, traders, costermongers, prostitutes, fish wives. The RANTER sings.

ENFRANCHISE ME

WHEN ADAM DELVED AND EVE SPAN
WHERE WAS THEN THE GENTLEMAN?
FROM WHERE DID THE ENTITLED START TO CRAWL?
THESE LANDED MEN THAT GOT NO SHAME,
THE LONG AND SHORT – NOT IN MY NAME
THEIR PARLIAMENT DON'T STAND FOR ME AT ALL.

OH OH ENFRANCHISE ME
OH OH GIVE ME A CHOICE
OH OH ENFRANCHISE ME
ALL I WANT'S A VOICE.

FOR YEARS WE BATTLE FLOOD AND DROUGHT,
THE BASTARDS LEAVE US LESS THAN NOWT.
THEY TAKE OUR LAND AND THEN THEY ASK FOR RENT.
THE BETTER PART DECIDE WHAT'S WHAT
THE GREATER PART ACCEPT THEIR LOT
THE NINETY-NINE RULED BY THE ONE PERCENT.

OH OH ENFRANCHISE ME
OH OH GIVE ME A CHOICE
OH OH ENFRANCHISE ME
ALL I WANT'S A VOICE

TO SAY "ENOUGH, NO MORE STATE TRICKS."
REJECT THE VILLAINS' POLITICS.
TO SERVE NO ONE BUT HIM I CHOOSE.
I'VE LITTLE LEFT BUT LIFE TO LOSE.

OH OH ENFRANCHISE ME
OH OH GIVE ME A CHOICE
OH OH ENFRANCHISE ME

ALL I WANT'S A VOICE
ALL I WANT'S A VOICE
ALL I WANT'S A VOICE

SWEET LIPS is soliciting and propositioning soldiers.

SWEET LIPS: D'yer want me to polish your gun soldier boy?

SOLDIER: How much?

SWEET LIPS: By hand, a farthing; lips, an 'apenny; full fanny horizontal, three farthings; anal, a penny.

SOLDIER: By hand will suffice.

He gives her the gun.

SWEET LIPS: Why have you given me the gun?

SOLDIER: Sorry, I think there's been a misunderstanding.

Enter SIR JOHN with DURAND.

SIR JOHN: They're a funny looking lot, Hull folk. Tattooed, bald, unshaven. I couldn't commend the men either.

Enter CAPTAIN JACK at pace with CAPTAIN MOYER.

JACK: Father! Meet Achilles.

SIR JOHN: Congratulations on slaying Hector.

MOYER: Captain Moyer, sir. The arsenal is secure and well defended.

SIR JOHN: Do you know any arsenals anywhere where one can just wander in and take what you like?

MOYER: No sir.

SIR JOHN: Don't look so pleased with yourself then.

MOYER: Sir, there were four soldiers on each watch, and I've increased that number twofold.

SIR JOHN: Not enough. Each watch needs at least eight men.

DURAND: Father, twofold four is eight.

SIR JOHN: In Oxford maybe, but this is Hull. With how much ease can we defend this town Captain Moyer?

MOYER: 'ull is defended by the 'umber on the south and the river to the east.

SIR JOHN: What's the river called?

MOYER: The River 'ull.

SIR JOHN: Bit fancy.

MOYER: I've stationed batteries before the Myton, Beverley, and North Gates, and the forts on the East of the river are all armed with canon.

SIR JOHN: Good, well done, take the week off.

JACK: No father, there is no respite! There is a cuckoo in the nest.

SIR JOHN: A cuckoo?

JACK: The King's feared and bloodthirsty cavalry officer, Prince Rupert, the royalist commander of horse, is in town, somewhere, hiding.

SIR JOHN: Hide and seek, and the other fellah's got a horse. Shouldn't be too difficult.

MOYER: They say he can kill a man with his bare feet.

JACK: During the thirty years war, abandoned and starving in a dungeon he ate a human liver to survive.

SIR JOHN: His own or someone else's?

MOYER: His first priority is to capture the arsenal, or, failing that, he might deny the use of the munitions by Parliament with the use of incendiaries.

SIR JOHN: Or, a third option, he might set fire to it.

MOYER: Yes sir.

SIR JOHN: What would happen to eighteen tons of gunpowder in a fire?

MOYER: We'd all be blown to hell and back sir.

SIR JOHN: You can come back, I'm not.

MOYER: The English Civil War could start today, in Hull. If Rupert –

SIR JOHN: – What does he look like?

MOYER: He's German sir, bit of a dandy, wears feathers.

SIR JOHN: Just feathers? Nothing else?

MOYER: Feathers as decoration.

JACK: Can I kill him father?!

DURAND: We are not at war.

SIR JOHN: Secure him.

JACK: But if he resists, can I kill him?

SIR JOHN: Alright yes! If you must! But don't tell your mother.

CAPTAIN JACK heads off in search of RUPERT.

DURAND: *(To MOYER.)* Where's Newcastle?

SIR JOHN: It's a small failing port on the River Tyne.

MOYER: The Royalist Earl of Newcastle with six hundred horse and a thousand foot is camped twenty miles north of Hull. He'll be pillaging your estate at Beverley before dusk.

DURAND: Nego consequentium! Prior to the outbreak of hostilities, any violation of property is an act of villainy and the perpetrator subject to arrest and the judicial process.

SIR JOHN: No gentleman can touch any of my sheep for meat or pleasure!

DURAND: Between King and Parliament how does the town incline?

MOYER: Seven thousand citizens, a dangerous number of masterless men, thrown off common land and ignited by the ideas of the age. All of Hull is in a wild humour. Ranters, Levellers, Millenarians.

SIR JOHN: We all need hats.

MOYER: In any dozen men there will be nine for the King.

SIR JOHN: What about the other four?

DURAND: Three.

SIR JOHN: The other three are villains are they?

MOYER: Villains sir? They're for Parliament. Like you and I.

SIR JOHN: Forgive me Captain Moyer, a trap to test your loyalty.

MOYER: The town objects to the billeting of our Parliament troops.

SIR JOHN: Have you not paid them?!

MOYER: John Pym has furnished you with funds for this cause has he not?

SIR JOHN: Not a penny. How much is the billeting each month?

MOYER: A thousand pounds.

DURAND: Father, it would serve us if we invented an outside threat, a rumour, to encourage the people to house the soldiers willingly.

SIR JOHN: Who do Hull folk hate most?

MOYER: People coming in from Beverley telling them what to do.

SIR JOHN: What else?

MOYER: The Pope, Spain, and buggery.

SIR JOHN: You! Come here.

A local comes over. SIR JOHN slips him a coin.

The King's papist wife approaches from Beverley with three thousand *Spanish* rape attack monks intent on sodomising any who objects to the quartering of Parliament troops. Pass it on.

He pushes him/her off. SWEET LIPS approaches HOTHAM.

SWEET LIPS: D'yer wanna girl?

SIR JOHN: No thank you.

SWEET LIPS: Two girls?

SIR JOHN: No.

SWEET LIPS: A boy?

SIR JOHN: What happened to three girls?

MOYER: This is Sweet Lips.

SWEET LIPS: You're Sir John Hot Hams aren't yer?

MOYER: You can't speak to the governor like that.

SWEET LIPS: Oh I can! The world's turned upside down. There's plots against you!

SIR JOHN: A Royalist bounty on my head?

SWEET LIPS: I were pleasing a Lord Cavalier, last night, outside the walls.

SIR JOHN: One of the Earl of Newcastle's men? What was he like?

SWEET LIPS: Very quick.

SWEET LIPS slopes off.

MOYER: Should I have her thrown out of the town sir?

SIR JOHN: Heavens no man! She's magnificent!

MOYER: These are puritan times sir. The London theatres are closed.

SIR JOHN: She is what theatre could be. She reaches out into the community, satisfying the real needs of her diverse clients. She's not an expensive building open six times a week and twice on Wednesdays.

MOYER: You're not of like mind then with John Pym on matters of Godliness?

SIR JOHN: The damned Puritans are madmen and fanatics! Can you think of anything more dangerous than everyone being able to read the Bible?!

MOYER: Out of uniform, I'm a Puritan lay preacher.

SIR JOHN: As am I. The very instigator of the Protestant Reformation, John Calvin is a personal friend of mine.

MOYER: He's dead.

SIR JOHN: And on his death bed he gave me this.

SIR JOHN pulls a biscuit out of his pocket.

MOYER: A biscuit?

SIR JOHN: His *personal* biscuit. Can you see, look, the face of the Virgin Mary.

MOYER: A relic? But Calvin was against the worship of icons.

SIR JOHN: *(Beat.)* Which is why he gave it to me.

Two trained bandsmen drag a CAVALIER along beating him furiously.

MOYER: Who is he?

SOLDIER: Spy for the King. Armed near Beverley Gate.

MOYER: Put him on the rack. We need to find Prince Rupert.

The soldiers drag the CAVALIER off roughly.

CAVALIER: Not the face!

Enter SARAH and JOHN SALTMARSH. SARAH, seeing SIR JOHN, holds back SALTMARSH.

SIR JOHN: So, if you're Achilles, and Hull is Troy, who am I?

DURAND: Helen.

SIR JOHN: What happened to her?

DURAND: Raped by Paris. I hope to find a book shop.

DURAND goes off on his own.

MOYER: Would you like a tour of the defences?

SIR JOHN: Excellent!

SIR JOHN and MOYER exit.

SALTMARSH: What is the sum of his commissions?

SARAH: A thousand from each, in coin. In two bags.

SALTMARSH: Sarah, two thousand could save my community and give you a new life with me, as an equal in the Family of Love.

SARAH: As your wife?

SALTMARSH: As one of my wives. Women are brethren and saints in my church.

SARAH: I don't want to be a wife of any kind ever again.

SALTMARSH: Then be a lover, and take other men as lovers in the Family. England is in flux. Together we can create that state of innocence before Adam's fall.

SARAH: But the money is promised to Pelham as a dowry for Frances.

SALTMARSH: But Pelham warmed to you more than your daughter?

SARAH: Around me his passion is unfettered.

SALTMARSH: His eagerness is manifest, in his hose?

SARAH: I may be wrong, it could be a ferret.

SALTMARSH: This is excellent. Tempt Pelham further, and his indiscretion might cause the marriage to founder, and the dowry will be our flotsam.

SARAH: Seduce and steal?!

SALTMARSH: Sin did not exist before Adam's fall! Men and women were equal and all property was held in common and that is how we shall live!

Enter LORD MAYOR BARNARD, searching.

Watch out! The Mayor! He's threatened to bar me from within the walls.

They scatter. THE MAYOR approaches SWEET LIPS.

SWEET LIPS: Percy!

BARNARD: Don't call me Percy in public, I'm the 'kin Mayor. Sweet Lips, 'ave yer seen two o' King's men. Military men, fearsome looking. They wan't where I arranged to meet 'em, undercover.

SWEET LIPS: They've not been under my covers.

Enter PRINCE RUPERT and the DUKE OF YORK. They are a pair of dandies essentially, with no trace of any military threat.

YORK: Lord Mayor Barnard?

BARNARD: Aye. What do you lads want? I'm busy.

YORK: James, Duke of York.

BARNARD: 'kinnel! Your majesty. I were expecting, you know, soldiers, not .. I mean I wouldn't wear that 'at in 'ull. And who –

RUPERT: – Ruprecht Pfalzgraf bei Rhein, Herzog von Bayern!

BARNARD: 'kinnel! And you're the terrifying Cavalier general of horse?

RUPERT: With the right horse, I am very scary.

This volley attracts the interest of a few local Parliament trained band members.

BARNARD: Shhh! Keep yer cake 'ole buttoned when –

RUPERT: – "cake 'ole"?

YORK: Mouth?

BARNARD: Aye! *(Finger to his lips.)*...when yer on the rerd.

RUPERT/YORK: The rerd?

BARNARD: The rerd!

YORK: Oh, the road!

BARNARD: Aye! And why wan't yer in the tenfoot as arranged?

YORK: We didn't know what a tenfoot was.

BARNARD: The alley down back o' the houses, usually ten foot wide.

BOTH: Oh!

BARNARD: And 'ave yer worked out 'ow the two of yer, on yer tod, are gonna capture an arsenal guarded by eight 'undred men?

YORK: The strategy I explained in my letter. Which is dependent on the loyalty of the citizens.

RUPERT: We storm the garrison, unter cover of dark, supported by the people, and invite the night watch to obey their King.

YORK: Have you informed the aldermen of this plan?

BARNARD: Aye, I terldamerl.

RUPERT: Was!?

BARNARD: I terldermerl!

YORK: I told them all?

BARNARD: Aye.

TRAINED BAND: *(Aggressively.)* Oi! Are you lads fer the perp?

RUPERT/YORK: The perp?

BARNARD: The 'ead o' Catholic church.

YORK: No! Papist scum. Boo.

RUPERT: Ja! We pass urine on Catholics.

> *The local retreats.*

BARNARD: Yer gonna have to lern yersen some 'ull and hide yersens an'all.

YORK: Disguises?

BARNARD: This is the English Civil War not a ruddy London masque!

> *BARNARD exits. Enter FRANCES. She is running, carrying letters, looking lost.*

YORK: Miss! You look lost!? Can we help?

FRANCES: Eurgh! We've just got here, and...and there's no messenger service!

YORK: *(Giving a card.)* This messenger is a shilling a month.

FRANCES: *(Aside.)* Oh! He's gorgeous!

RUPERT: Unlimited letters.

FRANCES: *(Aside.)* And his friend is gorgeous too. And a bit bigger! Frances Hotham

YORK: Are you Hotham's daughter?

FRANCES: Yes, I'm the middle child. Ninth out of seventeen.

YORK: Is that a Shakespeare quarto you're reading?

FRANCES: Yes. Romeo.

YORK: And Juliet?

FRANCES: I don't know, I've just started it.

> *She looks at cover.*

Oh yes.

YORK: They both die.

FRANCES: Deurgghhh!

YORK: Don't read it. It would be a tragedy for such a fair lily to fear love. Read one of his comedies.

FRANCES: Is love nothing sir?

YORK: To me, love is everything.

FRANCES: *(Aside.)* Ohhh!

YORK: Do you write letters?

FRANCES: Yeah.

YORK: This is my address.

FRANCES: James at Mayor's house, Hull.

RUPERT: Rupert at mayor's house, Hull.

FRANCES: All upper case?

RUPERT: I'm German.

FRANCES: *(Offers her card.)* Frances Hotham, at Governor's House, Hull.

YORK: *(To FRANCES.)* Do you ride?

FRANCES: Yeah. Mainly horses.

YORK: Tomorrow?

FRANCES: Ohhh. Yes.

> *DURAND approaches.*

DURAND: Sister! Alone? Out here!? The streets are teeming with soldiers.

FRANCES: I know.

YORK: We mean your sister no harm, we are innocently debating the merits of Romeo and Juliet.

DURAND: A ridiculous play. Two wholly unsuitable *children*, both fantastically shallow and ignorant – both of each other, and how the world works – utterly selfish, choose to throw themselves under the cart of love.

RUPERT: You have never met the right girl.

DURAND: I have met several girls in Beverley and found them all ridiculous.

YORK: Are you never transported by a woman's beauty?

DURAND: Beauty does not exist. It is culturally defined, a series of learned constructs.

YORK: *(Aside.)* I shall stake this cold raisonneur's heart and then tup his sister.

First you dismiss love. Then you banish love's first lieutenant, beauty.

DURAND: A small nose is admired. Why not condemn it as weak? It only needs society to decide that large noses are the height of loveliness and then a nose the size of St. Paul's would delight everyone.

YORK: What of your own heart? Does it never leap?

DURAND: The circulationists tell us that the heart is a muscle and its function is to deliver blood to the extremities of the body. The heart has no amorous vocation. It is a pump.

YORK: Then sir, I hope you have a long and rational life and that you never suffer a broken pump.

DURAND exits.

RUPERT: If we are to wear disguises, can I be ein mädchen? Please.

YORK: Yes. We will make a fine pair of wenches.

Enter, upstage, CAPTAIN JACK.

RUPERT: Achtung! A Parliament officer!

FRANCES: My big half brother, also called John Hotham, but we call him Captain Jack, because he asked us to, at knifepoint.

YORK: I'll send you a letter.

RUPERT: Ich auch!

FRANCES: *(Aside.)* I am struck! Twice! Opened by the softness, and charm of one, and hopelessly pinned by the bigger man's uniform.

JACK: Sister! What are you doing? Alone in the streets with all these soldiers about? A lone mouse amongst a thousand hungry hawks.

FRANCES: If only.

She runs off. Enter MOYER and SIR JOHN.

MOYER: You and your family will be safe here at the Governor's house. I'll post a marine on the door.

SIR JOHN: It's a fine house, would make a good pub.

MOYER: It's very secure as it also houses the strong boxes for the town. Do you believe in ghosts?

SIR JOHN: Captain Moyer, I'm a rational man. I don't fear the supernatural.

MOYER: They say it is a child, murdered by her father for breaking a vase. She wanders the stairs at night.

SIR JOHN: Is there nowhere else we can stay?

Beat of a drum and in come the Family of Love singing.

SONG

FAMILY:
THE POWER OF LOVE IS TRULY AWESOME
TRULY AWESOME, TRULY AWESOME,
THE POWER OF LOVE IS TRULY AWESOME
AND HE GAVE US SIN TO SAVE OUR SOULS

DID YOU KNOW SINNERS THAT SIN CAN MAKE YOU HAPPY
SIN CAN MAKE YOU HAPPY, SIN CAN MAKE YOU HAPPY
DID YOU KNOW SINNERS THAT SIN CAN MAKE YOU HAPPY
AND YOU DON'T HAVE TO GO TO CHURCH

LOCAL: Don't you mean "he gave *his son* to save our souls?"

SALTMARSH: No. He gave *us sin.* Judgement is finished and sin is victorious! Only the libertine can achieve heaven! And who can judge the libertine?

FAMILY MEMBER: God?

SALTMARSH: Not God, for God created sin! Sin is God's work! So sin some! And sin some more! And sin again!

SIR JOHN: If Jesus Christ had preached that kind of doctrine they'd have crucified him.

MOYER: They did.

SIR JOHN: Well, there you go then.

> *SIR JOHN goes in, shutting out the CAPTAIN. SALTMARSH stands on a milking stool.*

MOYER: What say you of adultery?

SALTMARSH: Adultery is the path to enlightenment! Join The Family of Love, and together we can build a new Eden here on the Humber. Bring your wives!

LOCAL: Where exactly is this new paradise?

SALTMARSH: North Ferriby.

MOYER: Where is God in all of this?

SALTMARSH: God is in the wood of your pipe Captain, and in the brass of your corset ma'am.

CALVERT: Why don't I have to go to church no more?

SALTMARSH: Because the horn you wake with on a Sunday, that is your steeple! Do not baptise your children, do not pay your tithes, reject war!

LOCAL: What about drinking?

SALTMARSH: One drink is good, two saintly, three divine, but getting totally shit faced every night, that is the true path to the Lord!

LOCAL: Where do we sign up?

SALTMARSH: Come with us, and give your love freely. The light of God has risen on the Humber!

FAMILY:
> JESUS LOVES YOU IF YOU GO 'ROUND THIEVING,
> GO 'ROUND THIEVING, GO 'ROUND THIEVING.
> JESUS LOVES YOU IF YOU GO 'ROUND THIEVING
> 'CAUSE GOD HELPS THOSE WHO HELP THEMSELVES.

END OF SCENE

SCENE TWO

Hull. Inside the Governor's House. Baskets of linen. A trunk set down stage. A hatch/trap to the coal cellar down stage. On the fireplace, either side a knight's helmet and broad sword. Enter CONNIE from the coal cellar. A vase set on a low table.

SARAH: Are you happy sleeping in the coal cellar Connie?

CONNIE: *(Mumbles at length her inaudible discontent.)*

SARAH: Don't mumble!

CONNIE: *(Mumbles more.)*

SARAH: I asked you a question!

CONNIE: *(Loud.)* I'm as happy as a flea on a nun's muff!

SARAH: For God's sake go back to mumbling. Have you seen Drudge?

CONNIE: No! He's so lazy he wouldn't pull a soldier off his own mother.

SARAH: Take this linen into the master bedroom. But don't look at the bed.

CONNIE: Don't look at the bed?

SARAH: A creation by the theatre designer Inigo Jones, it is… affecting.

CONNIE: Built a theatre of loving has he?

SARAH: Indeed.

> *CONNIE exits to the bedroom leaving the door open.*

CONNIE: *(Off.)* Bloody 'ell!

SARAH: Drudge!

> *DRUDGE opens the trunk with the vase on it, and climbs out. The vase hits the floor but does not break.*

SARAH: Must be unbreakable stoneware.

DRUDGE tries to break it. FRANCES opens the door to the bedroom stage right.

FRANCES: Please mummy! Could I have this room overlooking the street! There's a quarterlight and if I stand on a chair I can see men!

FRANCES closes the door. Enter SIR JOHN.

SIR JOHN: There's a plot against my life!

SARAH: I've never made a secret of it.

SIR JOHN: Royalists. Connie a glass of porter!

CONNIE organises the porter.

Drudge!? Listen! Someone may poison my food or drink so you need to taste it before I do. That way you die not me, which is better for everyone, because I'm a gentleman and you're an idiot. Understand?

CONNIE delivers the glass of porter, SIR JOHN takes it, DRUDGE takes it out of his hand and drinks down in one leaving nothing, and gives it back to him. CONNIE tops it up, and DRUDGE drinks it all again. And throughout the scene where possible.

SARAH: Mr Pelham will arrive shortly to collect his dowry. Where is it?

SIR JOHN: I've locked it in a safe box in the bedroom.

SARAH: You have the key?

SIR JOHN: Around my neck.

Knock at the door. SIR JOHN opens the door.

You're not Mr Pelham?

BARNARD: Henry Barnard.

SIR JOHN: Who are you and what do you want?

BARNARD: I'm the rightly elected Lord Mayor of 'ull.

SIR JOHN: By nepotism, favours and influence. I am Sir John Hotham, appointed governor of Hull by Parliament, ergo, you're a pint pot of piss and I'm the ocean.

BARNARD: Parliament dun't mean nowt to the 'ull mob, none of them gorra vote.

SIR JOHN: You love the King –

BARNARD: – aye.

SIR JOHN: As do I.

BARNARD: Grand! Burr I were told, you was appointed by John Pym to secure the arsenal for Parliament.

SIR JOHN: Correct, but at an opportune time, I will hand it over to the King to further his cause, which is my cause, which is your cause, which is his cause.

SARAH: My husband was knighted by Charles's father, James, and is loyal to the Stuarts.

SIR JOHN: Sarah? What are you doing?

SARAH: Participating –

SIR JOHN: – in matters of state!? Find some women's work. Wash a pony or shave your back!

> *SARAH exits.*

I apologise for my wife's exaggerated opinion of her own abilities.

BARNARD: I wanna see yer orders!

SIR JOHN: *(To DURAND.)* The letter from John Pym.

> *DURAND opens the letter and reads.*

DURAND: "Sir John Hotham, knight –

SIR JOHN: – that's me.

DURAND: – shall secure Hull and ensure that no English or other forces whatsoever, be suffered to enter. In the doing whereof the Mayor –

SIR JOHN: – that's you.

DURAND: – is commanded to assist the governor –

SIR JOHN: – that's me.

DURAND: – or he –

BARNARD: – me?

HOTHAM: No, I think that's me again.

DURAND: Will answer to the governor –

BARNARD: No! That me was me not you!

DURAND: – and Parliament at his peril."

SIR JOHN: That's your peril.

BARNARD: My peril?

SIR JOHN: Yes! And peril can mean anything up to and including execution.

BARNARD: I ant done owt yit!

SIR JOHN: I shall protect you.

BARNARD: Are yer gonna welcome Charles into the town then?

SIR JOHN: Charles who?

BARNARD: Charles Stuart, the king! He's coming to 'ull.

SIR JOHN: What?!

DURAND: The King comes to Hull?!

BARNARD: At first light!

SIR JOHN: *(Aside.)* Sodom and tomorrow!

To comply with my orders I shall have to bar the king.

BARNARD: Bugger me! I'll go t' foot of our stairs! No man has ever denied an English King and kept his 'ead!

SIR JOHN: My heart is for the King.

BARNARD: But yer signature is on Parliament parchments.

SIR JOHN: Ink! What is ink to blood?

BARNARD: 'appen as mebbe but I'm gonna send his son round. Yer can explain to the prince why yer might choose to bar his father.

SIR JOHN: The King's son is here in Hull?

BARNARD: The Duke of York, aye. Now I have summat to thrash out wi' you.

SIR JOHN: We both have concerns.

BARNARD: Bags foggy!

SIR JOHN: Eh?!

BARNARD: I'll go fost. Where's the thousand pound what John Pym give yer for the billeting o' these bastard roundheads?

SIR JOHN: The money is being weighed. In London. It arrives tomorrow.

BARNARD: Pay the mob or I fear for your life. They're west Hull lads. Everything's, you know, black and white.

SIR JOHN: Consider it done. Now my concern. We – what's your first name?

BARNARD: Percy.

SIR JOHN: What a lovely name.

BARNARD: Ta.

SIR JOHN: Percy, my duplicity must remain a strict confidence, or Captain Moyer and Parliament will have my head.

BARNARD hugs HOTHAM.

BARNARD: We're brothers! Long live the King!

SIR JOHN: Long live the King!

BARNARD leaves. SIR JOHN slams the door on him.

SIR JOHN: Charles comes to Hull tomorrow!

SARAH enters.

SARAH: Why did you say we could pay for the billeting? We've promised that money to Pelham for the dowry!

SIR JOHN: Thank you for reminding me! Where would I be without you, you barren, Saphic aspirant.

SARAH: In heaven, prick for brains.

SIR JOHN: Cavern fadged, dildo breaker.

SARAH: Under cocked, Norfolk arsed, wind manufactory.

SARAH exits.

DURAND: *(Aside.)* All I know of love, I know from these two.

SIR JOHN: *(Aside.)* My King comes to Hull, to take the arsenal, his arsenal. And I am aligned against him, opposed, antagonistic, ornery. A mortal man versus God's agent. Am I thus antithetical to God? Oh dear, what have I done.

> *Knock at door. SARAH returns but FRANCES runs out, opens it and takes two letters off a messenger and gives back two more before returning to her room.*

DURAND: Father, it might be prudent to use the Parliament money for the billeting and delay Frances's marriage.

SIR JOHN: No!

DURAND: I fear the mob.

SARAH: No!

SIR JOHN: We only have to raise a thousand. *(To SARAH.)* Give me your jewellery!

> *Grabbing the necklace around her throat.*

SARAH: You'll have to kill me first.

SIR JOHN: Drudge! Knife!

> *DRUDGE produces a knife. SARAH knees SIR JOHN in the balls. He collapses. SARAH exits to the main bedroom.*

CONNIE: Stay calm my sweet.

SIR JOHN: I can't cope.

CONNIE: You can. You've got me.

SIR JOHN: I would swap everything for a commoner's cottage and you.

CONNIE: Aye well, enclosure's done for that.

SIR JOHN: How can a man ride two horses at once?

CONNIE: Parliament is the instrument of the King. If you declare for the King's instrument, then you are both for the King and his instrument, Parliament.

SIR JOHN: Brilliant! Such wisdom! Such buzzwams!

> *He squeezes her breasts. Enter SARAH. She sees this action.*
> *HOTHAM fakes rubbing dust off her smock.*

SARAH: There's a money lender across the road. Connie, get him to visit Sir John.

> *CONNIE exits.*

SIR JOHN: Oh brilliant! I'm going to be in hock to Shylock of Hull!

SARAH: He's called Albert Calvert.

DURAND: He doesn't sound Jewish.

SIR JOHN: Did Jesus?

SARAH: Did Jesus what?

SIR JOHN: Sound Jewish.

SARAH: Jesus Christ?

SIR JOHN: Doesn't sound Jewish does it? They change their names to fit in. Fischman / Fisher; Herschel / Hurst; Ashkenazi / Albert Calvert.

SARAH: What are you saying?

SIR JOHN: That Jesus Christ was probably called Moshe Cohen before he moved to Jerusalem!

Knock at the door.

Argh!

DURAND: That might be the Duke of York.

SARAH opens it to PEREGRINE PELHAM. He is carrying books and some meat wrapped in bloodied paper.

SARAH: Mister Pelham!

She offers her hand to kiss.

PELHAM: I must divert my eyes from your perfect hand. All the sins can make use of a woman's fingers.

SARAH: I could wear a glove.

He hands over the bloodied meat wrapper.

PELHAM: For you madam, a gift.

SARAH: What lovely paper. What is it?

PELHAM: Pork.

SARAH: Loin.

PELHAM: Shoulder.

SARAH: Bone in.

PELHAM: Are you offended? I could take it out.

SARAH: No, no I like a bone in.

Enter DRUDGE from below with a hammer. He leaves the hatch open. He attacks the vase.

SIR JOHN: Drudge! Stop that. Come here!

SIR JOHN picks DRUDGE up and drops him down the cellar steps, and kicks the hatch closed.

SARAH: And you have brought your library with you sir?

PELHAM: Reading, for your daughter's improvement. Foxe's book of Martyrs; The Practice of Piety; A Way in Prayer; and my favourite, "Sin".

SIR JOHN: My favourite sin? Lust. Every time. What's yours?

PELHAM: My favourite book, "Sin".

SIR JOHN: Ah!

SARAH: Be assured this is a Puritan house.

SIR JOHN: Of which John Pym would approve. Our only recreation is the mortification of the flesh, and on Tuesdays self-flagellation.

SARAH: Sir John and I abstain from all physical pleasures.

SIR JOHN: Seeking that pure state of misery known as marriage.

Enter FRANCES from the master bedroom.

FRANCES: Oooh. I've just seen the bed! Have you seen the bed?! Oooh.

SARAH: Frances! Come and sit with your future husband.

FRANCES: Eeurgh yuk!

FRANCES runs up to her room.

SIR JOHN: When she really likes someone she goes yuk and runs to her room.

DURAND offers his hand as introduction.

My son, Durand. He's a lawyer, and tedious with it.

DURAND: The marriage contract.

PELHAM: Tedious but useful.

DURAND gives PELHAM a document.

PELHAM: And the dowry?

SIR JOHN: *(To DURAND giving him the key.)* Bring Mister Pelham's dowry from the safe box in the master bedroom.

PELHAM: Will Frances not sit with us?

SARAH: She is disturbed by sighting the Inigo Jones bed.

PELHAM: I hear that one only has to look at it and one imagines the beast with two backs.

SIR JOHN: Two, three, or four backs.

SARAH: As Puritans ourselves, we're having it turned into kindling.

PELHAM: Is it an aphrodisiac?

SIR JOHN: Kindling, no, we use it to get the fire going.

> *Enter DURAND with the two money bags. DURAND then offers PELHAM a quill. He leaves the safe box key on the desk. SARAH sees this and moves towards it.*

The dowry, two thousand in coin, as promised, and contracts.

PELHAM: Excellent.

> *PELHAM signs and passes the contract to SIR JOHN. When they're busy signing, SARAH surreptitiously takes the key and sticks it in her bosom. PELHAM takes both money bags and sits holding them. Enter CONNIE from the street.*

CONNIE: The money lender says he will call in shortly.

PELHAM: You're borrowing money?

SARAH: No! Usury is a sin!

SIR JOHN: Why would I want to see the money lender?

SARAH: To close him down.

SIR JOHN: I am ending his reign! We cannot have the citizens of Hull tempted by Mammon.

PELHAM: I saw the mayor leaving. What do I tell John Pym about you associating with Royalists and Papists? You know he has a proper priest's hole?

SIR JOHN: I didn't. Our only intimacy has been a handshake.

PELHAM: The Duke of York and Prince Rupert are in Hull. Or so it is rumoured. It would advantage us and please Parliament if they were arrested.

DURAND: But we are not at war, yet, by law they are but Englishmen and free.

PELHAM: Prince Rupert is German.

SIR JOHN: So an Englishman and a Germanman, but both free.

PELHAM: You speak as if you have some sympathy with the malignant party.

SIR JOHN: No, no, no.

DURAND: The malignant party? That phrase has no inherent meaning.

PELHAM: The royalists.

DURAND: If you were a royalist, *malignant party,* would mean Parliament. Ergo, the words "malignant" and "party" are empty vessels waiting to be filled with meaning by others cognisant of your own position.

SIR JOHN: You're not marrying him.

DURAND: The use of such solipsistic patter is lazy, vain and self-gratifying.

PELHAM stands, insulted.

SARAH: You'll only see him at Christmas!

SIR JOHN: He's a mere barnacle on a beautiful ship! Our two families bound in bondage! My fecund estates and your gold!

PELHAM: I've heard you shit off the bridge.

SIR JOHN: Completely untrue! But I make a pledge to you, I'll never do it again.

Door knocker. CONNIE opens it. MR CALVERT is there.

CALVERT: Albert Calvert. I'm told you require a loan?

SIR JOHN: A story, I concocted to contrive this three way conjunction. You know Mr Pelham?

CALVERT: Aye, that damned Puritan's been trying to close me down for six years.

SIR JOHN: And in that, as in religion, and politics, he and I are united. No longer shall I permit you to flaunt your balls in public.

CALVERT: I'm a freeborn Englishman.

SIR JOHN: Oh suddenly you're English are you?!

CALVERT: Born and bloody bred, aye. Where's the law in this?

DURAND: Jus est, ars boni.

CALVERT: First it's mi balls, and now it's mi arse.

DURAND: The law – jus – is the art – ars – of what is good – boni.

CALVERT: And what does the law say about the two hornifying soldiers tekking ovver mi house, eating mi food, and contriving new experiences for mi daughters? Without no compensation!

SIR JOHN: You will be remunerated in full for the billeting of troops. Tomorrow.

> *Door knocker knocks twice. SIR JOHN opens the door, looks out.*

SIR JOHN: Argh!

> *He closes the door. SIR JOHN draws his sword.*

SIR JOHN: Durand! Take refuge in your room!

CALVERT: Do you arrest me?!

SIR JOHN: No! Behind that door stand the King's son, the Duke of York, and Prince Rupert. I have tricked them into visiting me here so that I can arrest all three of them.

PELHAM: Two. The Duke of York and the King's son is one and the same person.

SIR JOHN: Good, that should make it easier.

> *DURAND goes up to his room. Knocking louder, and with impatience. PELHAM stands, holding the money bags.*

PELHAM: You plan to arrest the Cavaliers with violence?

SIR JOHN: I know the merit of force, whilst respecting the dangers.

CALVERT: I'm loyal to the King. Don't look to me for service.

SIR JOHN: But you cannot leave, so protect yourself. Get in the trunk!

CALVERT: I will not!

PELHAM: Prince Rupert is known for his intemperate will. If war breaks out in this room you will not have time to explain your allegiances.

> *CALVERT gets in the trunk.*

SIR JOHN: Drudge!

> *DRUDGE opens the hatch and comes up the stairs.*

Mr Pelham, hide your dowry in the coal cellar, these godless cavaliers see all gold as the spoils of war.

SARAH: – avec moi.

PELHAM: Enchanté.

> *SIR JOHN kicks the hatch shut trapping PELHAM's fingers.*

Aargh!

> *SIR JOHN gives DRUDGE a sword from the fireplace. DRUDGE takes the sword gift as an invitation to wear the helmet too, the visor of which blinds him and he goes around blindly attacking stuff including the vase. Further knocking.*

CONNIE: The door?

SIR JOHN: Don't let them in yet.

> *SIR JOHN lifts the trunk lid.*

SIR JOHN: *(Fierce whisper.)* Could you loan me a thousand?

CALVERT: But –

SIR JOHN: – everything I said before was for the benefit of that Puritan arseworm! How much would the charge be?

CALVERT: Thirty pounds in a hundred.

SIR JOHN: Thirty!? In a hundred!? That's nearly twenty-five percent! What's the rate for Jews?

CALVERT: I only have one rate.

SIR JOHN slams the lid down, trapping CALVERT's fingers.

CALVERT: Aargh!

He knocks out DRUDGE with the vase and hangs him on the hook where the helmet/sword combo was. SIR JOHN heads for the door. Enter DURAND from his room.

DURAND: Father!

SIR JOHN: Get back in your room! Connie! Stand on the hatch!

CONNIE stands on the hatch. FRANCES enters.

FRANCES: Father, what –

SIR JOHN: – get back in there you randy minx!

She doesn't, she watches. SIR JOHN opens the door, with a bow. Revealed are the DUKE OF YORK, and PRINCE RUPERT.

SIR JOHN: *(Fierce whisper.)* Shhhh!!! Your majesty, welcome.

YORK: May I present Prince Rupert of the Rhein.

SIR JOHN genuflects, on his knees.

SIR JOHN: Sir, welcome, I am your servant.

YORK: But, Hotham, you are retained by Parliament. Our warm welcome surely is not advised by John Pym?

SIR JOHN: No, this over buttered obsequiousness is mine own design.

> *Enter FRANCES down the stairs. She gives each of them a letter. YORK gives her a letter. RUPERT gives her a letter. She goes off and tears at the letter, devouring it.*

You know each other?

RUPERT: We use the same messaging service.

> *FRANCES mimes tearing her heart out and giving it to YORK. YORK mimes tearing his heart out and giving it to FRANCES.*

SIR JOHN: But listen! Your majesties, there is treachery for you within this house, an assassin! But I beg of you, humour me a lunatic pageant, think of it as a masque, it is in the service of your safety. *(Shouted.)* I COMMAND YOU! LAY DOWN YOUR ARMS OR YOUR LIFE, LIVES I SHALL CURTAIL!! FACE DOWN YOU GERMAN CAVALIER DOG!

> *RUPERT gets on his knees. SIR JOHN pulls him up.*

No, no. You don't have to do that.

AND YOU THE OTHER CAVALIER DOG!

> *YORK drops to his knees, but SIR JOHN jumps in with a whisper.*

SIR JOHN: *(Whisper.)* No, no, I will not harm you your majesty. YOU CHALLENGE ME! ERGO YOU FORFEIT YOUR LIFE!

> *SIR JOHN starts fencing DRUDGE's sword, just for the noise of it. Meanwhile FRANCES has opened RUPERT's letter and is now miming that she loves him too.*

AH! SOME WITTY GERMAN SWORDPLAY PRINCE RUPERT!

> *He attacks DRUDGE's sword, this time DRUDGE fences back, which amazes YORK and RUPERT who both draw their swords and prepare to attack DRUDGE.*

SIR JOHN: No, he's on our side.

SIR JOHN fences DRUDGE all the way to the trunk, takes his sword off him, sits him on the trunk.

Sit there, don't move.

Then he fences himself, ending up pinning himself against the wall with the two swords.

SIR JOHN: YOU HAVE ME! SPARE MY LIFE, I HAVE FIVE WIVES AND SEVENTEEN CHILDREN. *(Shouting at the closed hatch.)* I am hit! Arghh! I mean, arrgghh! I am hit!

More sword clattering.

HA HA THE TABLES TURN! LAY DOWN YOUR SWORD!

He throws a sword down.

SUBMIT! I SHALL NOT SHOW MERCY TO GERMAN PAPIST SCUM. Sorry Prince Rupert.

CALVERT opens the trunk lid quickly. DRUDGE remains on the lid unmoved, so ends up at 90 degrees to the floor. CALVERT is puzzled, expecting to see a cavalier pinned to the ground he sees SIR JOHN pointing his sword at the ground and the cavaliers up stage watching on. On seeing CALVERT both RUPERT and YORK draw their swords.

YORK: Assassin!

RUPERT: Preparen Sie to die noble sir!

As RUPERT and YORK step forward to kill CALVERT.

SIR JOHN: No! Nein!

SIR JOHN steps in and starts sword fighting YORK and RUPERT. CALVERT starts edging towards the door. Enter CAPTAIN JACK, who, seeing the two cavaliers with swords drawn, draws his own sword.

JACK: Prince Rupert! Assassins!

RUPERT: Nein! We are not assassins!

YORK: And we are not at war yet sir!

CAPTAIN JACK: And you're the King's son!

YORK: Is regicide your aim?

> *JACK charges the two cavaliers, who defend themselves. CALVERT escapes out the main door. Enter the child ghost, she picks up the vase. YORK and RUPERT are struck dumb. JACK stabs her through the neck and yet she is extant. She puts the vase back on the table, turns and walks into the master bedroom. RUPERT knocks out JACK with the vase.*

YORK: A soul in purgatory?

SIR JOHN: A girl murdered by her father for breaking a vase.

YORK: So our assassin is your own son?

> *RUPERT draws his sword again as if to murder JACK.*

SIR JOHN: No! Don't kill him, that is not my son Jack.

YORK: Prove it?

SIR JOHN: How old would you say this man is?

YORK: He's young.

RUPERT: Twenty-five?

SIR JOHN: Indeed, but Jack fought in the eighty years war and the thirty years war, so Jack is at least a hundred and ten.

RUPERT: Ich cannot argue mit das.

YORK: Sorry.

SIR JOHN: Now go! And disguise yourselves, for I shall tell Mister Pelham that you are both arrested and imprisoned by Captain Moyer.

> *YORK and RUPERT leave.*

Drudge! Go into Durand's room and kick and bang on the door. Make it sound like two men trying to break out.

DRUDGE goes up the stairs to DURAND's room, and starts banging on the door. SIR JOHN rubs meat blood on his shirt. DRUDGE goes in, and starts banging on the door.

SIR JOHN: You can come up now!

SIR JOHN opens the hatch. Enter SARAH and PELHAM up the stairs.

PELHAM: *(Fearful.)* Sir, you're bleeding heavens hard!

SIR JOHN: Ah, it'll wash out!

SARAH: Jack! Is he dead?

SIR JOHN: Unconscious, knocked out by that feathered German bedlamite.

PELHAM: *(Fearful.)* Where are the Cavaliers now?

SIR JOHN: Secure in that upstairs room, but as you can hear, they're trying to break out.

They listen, nothing.

AS YOU CAN HEAR, THEY'RE TRYING TO BREAK OUT!

DRUDGE starts banging violently.

I have locked the door, and it is secure for now, and Captain Moyer is called, but as you can tell their blood is up!

DRUDGE breaks a panel in the door and tumbles onto the balcony.

They took Drudge hostage with them! But he's escaped! Well done Drudge!

SIR JOHN draws his sword.

There is no time to lose! If you value your life sir, go now!

PELHAM: My money is hidden in the coal.

SIR JOHN: I'll secure it in the safe box.

PELHAM: But –

SIR JOHN: – It'll be safe under lock and key. The contract is signed, that is your money.

SARAH: Come and see me tomorrow, to collect.

> *PELHAM exits. The door closes, HOTHAM leans against the door, and breathes. SARAH heads for the hatch.*

SIR JOHN: Stop!

> *SARAH stops.*

Don't think I can't spot your game, you grasping dyke! Drudge, recover the money from the coal.

> *SARAH hands over the key and goes into the bedroom. SIR JOHN slips down the wall exhausted.*

CONNIE: My sweet muffin. Why did you rub meat on your shirt?

SIR JOHN: I have no feculent idea! Look at me, I'm sweating like a kestrel.

CONNIE: You're doing what any man would do. Protecting your family from the danger of ending the war on the wrong side.

> *SIR JOHN: Yes! At least you understand me Connie. The other Knight's helmet falls and lands on his head.*

END OF SCENE

Act Three

SCENE ONE

The day after. Outside the Beverley Gate, so the outer town wall is upstage. People throng and trade. SALTMARSH lurks. SWEET LIPS solicits. The drawbridge is down and the gate open. The RANTERS sing.

ENCLOSURE

THEY HANG THE MAN, AND FLOG THE WOMAN,
THAT STEALS THE GOOSE FROM OFF THE COMMON;
BUT LET THE GREATER VILLAIN LOOSE,
THAT STEALS THE COMMON FROM THE GOOSE.
THE LAW DEMANDS THAT WE ATONE
WHEN WE TAKE THINGS WE DO NOT OWN
BUT LEAVES THE LORDS AND LADIES FINE
WHO TAKES THINGS THAT ARE YOURS AND MINE AND…

ENCLOSURE TRAMPLES ALL THAT'S IN ITS WAY,
LEAVES THE POOR MAN A SLAVE.
ENCLOSURE, AND WE CAN'T DO SHIT BUT RANT AND RAVE
FENCED IN TIL THE GRAVE.

THE POOR AND WRETCHED DON'T ESCAPE
IF THEY CONSPIRE THE LAW TO BREAK;
THIS MUST BE SO BUT THEY ENDURE
THOSE WHO CONSPIRE TO MAKE THE LAW.
THEY HANG THE MAN, AND FLOG THE WOMAN
WHO STEALS THE GOOSE FROM OFF THE COMMON
AND GEESE WILL STILL A COMMON LACK
UNTIL WE GO AND STEAL IT BACK AND…

ENCLOSURE. THIS ENGLAND, THIS OUR COMMON LAND.
EARTH, MUD, CLAY AND SAND.
ENCLOSURE. NOW WE WATCH THESE BLOATED FARMS EXPAND.
SHALL WE NOT MAKE A STAND?
ENCLOSURE, SO RAIL AS THE RAILINGS RISE
OR WATCH THE COUNTRY'S DEMISE.
ENCLOSURE. NO ONE SELLING, SOMEONE BUYS

WHILE OLD ALBION DIES.
WHILE OLD ALBION DIES.

> *Enter CONNIE, she is collecting stones in an iron bucket so they make a noise.*

CONNIE: If a man denies a King
He himself a traitor makes
And every high born noble man
Sleeps ill, and every landless man wakes

And God has shown us revolution
In the garden way back when
When Adam delved and Eve span
Where then was the gentleman?

> *Enter SARAH who is approached by SALTMARSH.*

SALTMARSH: Turnip!

SARAH: Parsnip, my sweet!

> *They snog furiously, and SALTMARSH gropes her. People stop to watch.*

Not here.

> *They move a couple of yards and start again.*

Not here either.

SALTMARSH: Do you have good news?

SARAH: Sir John returned the money bags to the safe box in the bedroom of the governor's house.

SALTMARSH: So he has the key?

SARAH: Indeed.

SALTMARSH: Turnip, that is not good news.

SARAH: I made an impression in soap.

SALTMARSH: Of Sir John?

SARAH: Of the key!

One of the smiths I used to visit is forging a duplicate as we speak.

SALTMARSH: We must rescue the coin before the King arrests Sir John.

SARAH: What if the King does not constrain him?

SALTMARSH: How can a citizen challenge a King and not be detained?!

They move off. Enter RUPERT and YORK, both disguised as girls, with a barrow full of fish.

YORK: I always wanted to be a princess.

RUPERT: Mich auch. I used to dream of being locked in a tower, growing my hair, zen one day rescued, kissed, unt taken roughly from behind.

YORK: Hiding in plain sight as girls is our best policy. And we have promised to be here to meet Frances.

RUPERT: Do you love her cus?

YORK: I want her.

RUPERT: For a night, oder forever?

YORK: I know not which, but I shall have her.

RUPERT: Yet it is me she loves. I have more letters.

Showing a fist full of letters.

YORK: More maybe, but her letters to me are longer, and fulsome!

RUPERT: Perhaps she's mad.

YORK: Or in love with love.

DURAND is seen.

YORK: Now *he,* her brother, has got my blood up more than her.

RUPERT: You love him? Socratische? Pederastical?

YORK: Rupert, feelings of love are like a rainbow.

RUPERT: Are you saying that sexuality is a spectrum?

YORK: I love girls, exclusively. My love is red. The first colour of the rainbow. What are you Rupert? Orange? Yellow? Green? Blue?

RUPERT: Keep going.

YORK: Indigo? Violet?

RUPERT: I find Joan of Arc attractive.

YORK: Short hair, looks like a boy? Rupert, you're violet!

RUPERT: Was it so obvious?

YORK: You have an interest in fabrics and wall hangings.

RUPERT: Zat tells you nothing.

YORK: And you climbed into my bed last night and felt my arse.

RUPERT: Sheisse! I thought you were asleep.

>*SIR JOHN approaches the stall.*

Pass auf! Here comes the governor.

YORK: Haddock! Sea bass! Coalie! Cod!

RUPERT: Come on Mutter, sort it out!

SIR JOHN: Fair maid, are you German?

RUPERT: Ja, I followed the herring.

SIR JOHN: Which one?

RUPERT: Diese.

SIR JOHN: I shall buy it, if you continue to follow it. Will you?

RUPERT: Jawohl!

>*SIR JOHN buys the herring and puts it in his pocket suggestively. PELHAM approaches.*

PELHAM: Hotham! Are the two effeminate Cavalier dandies arrested?

RUPERT draws a dagger but YORK holds him back. SIR JOHN, and PELHAM promenade, out of earshot to YORK and RUPERT.

SIR JOHN: Imprisoned in the bilges of Captain Moyer's ship. You won't see them again, unless they escape.

PELHAM: And when is the King expected?

SIR JOHN: Eleven. But he's the King, so he can be late if he wants can't he, or not turn up at all. It's not a sensible way to run a country.

PELHAM: And I can trust you to bar his entrance?

SIR JOHN: My orders from Parliament are almost unequivocal.

PELHAM: Good. It will be an honour to have such a brave man as a father-in-law.

SIR JOHN: And I don't think of it as losing a daughter. I'm gaining a religious zealot.

PELHAM: There she is now. With your permission, I will engage with her.

SIR JOHN: Speak of love, it's her only subject.

PELHAM moves off. CAPTAIN MOYER enters.

SWEET LIPS: Lawrence! Lawrence!

MOYER: Not now mi sweet artichoke, I'm in uniform.

BARNARD approaches.

BARNARD: Hotham! I need to know, are yer gonna let the King in?

HOTHAM: I have my orders Lord Mayor.

BARNARD: 'ull folk are stomachful o' Parliament and nine out o' twelve of 'em are royalist.

CAPTAIN MOYER approaches threateningly.

SIR JOHN: Captain Moyer told me it's only three quarters.

BARNARD: Nine twelfths is three quarters!

SIR JOHN: Don't be ridiculous!

BARNARD: If yer divide nine by three, and twelve by three –

SIR JOHN: – let's just agree to differ!

BARNARD: If yer don't let the king in, and if yer continue to billet the soldiers without no compensation, well, the mob, they'll gerrodofyer and brae 'ell outa yer!

SIR JOHN: Brae?

BARNARD: Tear you limb from limb.

> *SIR JOHN whispers in BARNARD's ear, conscious of MOYER and others listening.*

SIR JOHN: Lord Mayor, I am loyal to my King, and what comes next is for show.

(To all.) The mob can gerrodome all they like! And when they do, and my limbs are scattered and my mind is just a grey blob of flesh pulsing in a tenfoot, then, even then, they shall not persuade me, for that blob is a blob of honour, in thrall to Parliament!

> *SIR JOHN storms off. FRANCES enters, holding her book.*

RUPERT: Fraulein, would you like to buy this cod?

FRANCES: Haddock. Dark blotch above the pectoral fin.

YORK: *What's in a name? That which we call a haddock. By any other word would smell as sweet.*

FRANCES: You mock me! Because I'm reading Romeo and Juliet!

YORK: I do not bite my thumb at you, dear lady.

FRANCES: Do you still bite your thumb?

YORK: A quote from the play.

FRANCES: Yes, I didn't understand that bit.

YORK: Does the play move you?

FRANCES: Like Juliet, I am tragically, hopelessly in love.

YORK: With whom?

FRANCES: A boy!

RUPERT: Is he good looking?

FRANCES: Ohhh yes! He's, ooooh, and he's really eeerghh!

YORK: – What do you feel for him?

FRANCES: Oooooh, nnnnnn, pheewwewe.

RUPERT: She's mad.

YORK: What would you do for him?

FRANCES: Everything.

YORK: Did you dream of him last night?

FRANCES: No, I dreamt of his cousin, with the uniform. Who
is equally handsome but is a bit bigger.

YORK: His cousin?! But his cousin is –

FRANCES: – bigger! Yes!

RUPERT: Tell us the dream.

FRANCES: I was shipwrecked on an island made of white linen
and I had no clothes on and there was a big horse wearing
a uniform, kneading dough, and I climbed on top of the
horse and then it rained and we both got wet. *(Beat.)* What
do you think it means?

> *YORK and RUPERT shake their heads as if clueless.*

YORK: But you love the other man too!?

FRANCES: I love them both. Urgh! But I am promised to that
Puritan there! Do you know a good way to kill yourself that
doesn't hurt?

> *They shake their heads. She runs off. YORK collapses to his
> knees.*

YORK: I am hit! Now that she is unattainable, I want her with
my life.

RUPERT: She loves me more.

YORK: Rupert, I am second in line to the English throne. What are you?

RUPERT: Eight hundred and seventh.

YORK: *And* you don't like girls. So cus, step aside.

RUPERT: What of my feelings?

YORK: You can dream of her brother.

RUPERT: And what about our commission, the taking or destruction of the arsenal?

YORK: All I know is that I am less inclined to take up arms in a Civil War than I am ripe to ride out and slay Durand and "his loveless party". But here's her future husband, my mortal enemy.

>   *PELHAM approaches.*

PELHAM: *(Averting his eyes.)* Have you no sense of decency. Cover your fish!

YORK: Whyfor sir?

PELHAM: So that they don't excite lewd thoughts!

>   *RUPERT covers the fish in a blanket, which leaves their heads showing.*

YORK: You are to be married soon Mr Pelham?

PELHAM: A man needs a wife.

YORK: To love, to adore, to worship?

PELHAM: To breed. The Lord said go forth and multiply, I can't do that on my own.

>   *PELHAM moves off.*

YORK: Another member of the loveless party. Let us declare war on them Rupert!

RUPERT: Jawohl!

YORK: Let us raze Durand's citadel of reason and then advance on Pelham's desert heart!

MESSENGER/SOLDIER at pace.

MESSENGER: *(Hull accent.)* Charlie's ower yonder now!

MOYER: Does the King have an army?

MESSENGER: Aye, I reckon near two hundred horse.

SIR JOHN: How many foot?

MESSENGER: 'bout fifty 'ead o' foot.

SIR JOHN: *(Aside/improvisation.) You madam! How many soldiers is fifty head of foot if every soldier has one head and two feet?*

Audience member: Fifty!

SIR JOHN: *Is that a guess or is it based on your own military experience?*

MESSENGER: I'm gerrin' inside!

MESSENGER runs within the walls.

SIR JOHN: Drudge! Stool!

DRUDGE forms himself into a stool and SIR JOHN stands on his back.

Citizens! I presume that everyone here would willingly lay down his life for the King.

General "ayes!". Followed by an isolated –

CITIZEN: – Wanker.

SIR JOHN: But only one subject here, is already commanded by the King, through his instrument, Parliament.

CITIZEN: Who's that then?

SIR JOHN: Tis I of whom I speak. And I shall not disobey Parliament, which is the King's instrument.

MOB: Boos / bollocks / you can't talk to us like that / I'm a yeoman / I done an apprenticeship / I gor an 'ouse / I was kicked off the common.

CITIZEN: Wanker.

SWEET LIPS: What are your orders Hot Hams?

SIR JOHN: As a loyal subject, to take all measures to protect His Majesty's Person if I foresee a danger to him from his own counsel.

SWEET LIPS: Yer gonna protect the King from his own generals?

SIR JOHN: We might witness here in Hull, today, the birth of constitutional parliamentary democracy. And what is needed at a birth is an experienced midwife with an oiled finger. I am that oily finger. But no baby can guarantee an easy birth –

SWEET LIPS: – it might have its head stuck the wrong way round.

SIR JOHN: Yes –

FEMALE CITIZEN: – our Dennis had 'is cord wrapped round its neck.

SIR JOHN: Yes! And –

MALE CITIZEN: – Might be twins!

SIR JOHN: No! No!

A trumpet sound near.

CITIZEN: Here's Charlie!

MOYER: Everyone! Within the walls! Draw the bridge!

The citizens rush to get within the walls as the drawbridge shows signs of rising.

BARNARD: You said you would allow the King access!

ALBERT CALVERT: Let the King in I say!

SWEET LIPS: And taste the pleasures!

The drawbridge starts to rise as the citizens scramble in behind the walls.

SIR JOHN: *(To the town crier.)* Announce the curfew as designed!

MOYER: CURFEW! CURFEW! CURFEW!

Everyone gets inside the walls.

CONNIE: Drudge! Drudge!

DRUDGE, who is standing one foot either side of the drawbridge as it rises is raised with the bridge, and then slips down on the inside. Enter the forward train of the King, cavaliers, foot soldiers, and then the King sat on a tiny white horse (a wooden prop) which is dirty with mud. The citizens are now standing on the walls looking down.

CHARLES: Announce my arrival.

A bugler plays a fanfare, Greensleeves.

SOLDIER 1: Oi! Keep the noise down I'm tryna have a lie in!

Laughter. The soldiers on the battlements pick up the tune and whistle it mockingly.

CHARLES: I am Charles Stuart, King of England.

SOLDIER 2: Go wipe your arse!

Laughter.

CHARLES: I wish to speak to the governor.

DIGGER: Who, with any wit, would choose a white horse?!

SOLDIER 2: There's a little shit showing on top.

CHARLES: Put me down!

CHARLES is picked off the horse by two soldiers. The white wooden horse is led off and as it goes it lifts its tail and shits.

And get this horse cleaned! Hotham! Why is this bridge raised up?!

SIR JOHN: According to your Majesty's orders.

CHARLES: I gave no such instruction.

SIR JOHN: Through your Parliament you did. Parliament is the instrument of the King, ergo you have ordered me not to let you in.

CHARLES: Duplicitous words Hotham!

SIR JOHN: Thank you!

CHARLES: Who the hell do you think you are?

SIR JOHN: A supplicant, and today it is a great honour for me to kneel before you, even in the lowly role of traitor.

CHARLES: Do you want to be the first dark cloud which will soon overspread this land and cast all into thunder?

SIR JOHN: I am not a dark cloud, I am a lovely day. You have here in Hull, not only a magazine of military provisions, but a magazine of hearts. The love that we feel for you is unbounded, and being unbounded it bounds everywhere in Hull's streets like an unbound hound of love.

CHARLES: The ordinance here is mine! Accumulated for the second Bishop's war.

SIR JOHN: Every last ounce of gunpowder is intact. I am merely protecting it for you.

CHARLES: Where's my son? The Duke of York. Have you detained him?

SIR JOHN: *(With a wink to MOYER.)* No, no. He's having breakfast.

CHARLES: It's eleven o'clock!?

SIR JOHN: Brunch.

CHARLES: Where's the mayor?

BARNARD: *(Off.)* Gissa skeg!

BARNARD's head shows above the parapet.

'ow do mi Liege, how glad I would have been to welcome you –

A soldier smacks him on the head and BARNARD collapses behind the walls.

CHARLES: This town –

ALL: – city!

CHARLES: This city is mine by name! Kingstown upon Hull. Show me your orders Hotham! Come out here with the document!

SIR JOHN: That cannot be done.

CHARLES: Why not?!

SIR JOHN: If they won't lower the gate for you, they're not going to let it down for me are they?

CHARLES: Throw him off the walls now!

SIR JOHN: No, that would be dangerous.

Uproar and fighting on the walls. BARNARD and another royalist alderman grab HOTHAM and try and throw him off the walls. DRUDGE and PELHAM fight back, and save SIR JOHN.

CHARLES: Proclaim the dog a traitor!

BUGLER plays fanfare. And SOLDIER puts the King back on a clean horse.

HERALD: Sir John Hotham, first baronet of Scorborough is a traitor, guilty of high treason, by order of Charles Stuart, King of England.

The King turns to go.

CHARLES: Leave this rat to his hole! I will have your head Hotham!

The King's train leave.

SIR JOHN: That went quite well.

END OF SCENE

INTERVAL

Act Four

SCENE ONE

Later that same day. The governor's house, main room. Enter DRUDGE with a huge log splitter maul. He heads for the vase and places it on the floor like a golf ball. He swings the maul and whacks it hard into the back wall. It doesn't break. The GHOST enters from the master bedroom and snatches up the vase.

GHOST: No sir! It's my vase.

> *DRUDGE tries to get the vase back.*

Mary Ascough. This vase is the last of a pair. I broke the other, which is why my father, drunk and enraged, killed me. My task in purgatory is to protect the vase, but in performing it, I cannot move on.

> *DRUDGE holds the vase like a baby.*

You will protect the vase? Then I am free and can be with God. It must not be broken, but if that happens then you must kill whoever breaks it.

> *Draws a knife and mimes defending the vase against all comers.*

DRUDGE: Ayyyyeeeaaaaa!

GHOST: Be diligent sir. I can now be with God.

> *The GHOST walks through a wall. Enter FRANCES and SARAH.*

> *DRUDGE is fiercer than ever.*

FRANCES: Is it right that we, the gentry, who own nine tenths of the land, are acquiring the rest by the aggressive enclosure of common pasture?

SARAH: Yes. Drudge! Put that knife down!

FRANCES: But it says here that the people have never endured such a painful yoke from foreign tyrants as from our own gentry – us. Why didn't anybody tell me that?

SARAH: You'd give everyone the vote would you?

FRANCES: Why not!?

SARAH: Imagine what kind of idiots would get elected.

FRANCES: When Adam delved, and Eve span, who then was the gentleman?

SARAH snatches a Diggers' pamphlet from FRANCES' hand. And looks at it.

SARAH: The Diggers!?

FRANCES goes into her room in a huff.

CONNIE: In times of turmoil masterless men crowd the streets like flies round a cow's –

SARAH: – go back to mumbling! I'm going to take advantage of the shops now that we're in Hull.

CONNIE: I was surprised there's no white bread bakers.

SARAH: I'm not interested in bread. Hats.

SARAH exits.

CONNIE: *(To DRUDGE.)* I'd like a bakers' shop. Master, mistress of my own destiny. Not wiping the –

Enter SIR JOHN and DURAND from the street.

SIR JOHN: – Connie! Where's the enemy?!

CONNIE: She found a hat shop.

SIR JOHN: Women!

(Aside.) I bar the King of England, I'm declared a traitor, certain death if the monarchy wins the war, and what does my wife do?! She goes shopping!

(Improvisation. Aside to a man with wife.) What's this one like? Eh? Any trouble? Fair. I suppose that's some compensation.

Heated banging on the door. DURAND opens it to BARNARD who storms in.

BARNARD: What mekks yer think yer can deny the King of England and live!? The image of Christ as God on earth!

SIR JOHN: If God's four foot nothing with a cleft palate God help us.

BARNARD: The folk of 'ull saw what yer done and they'll not wait no more now. They want their rightful money. For the billeting of troops.

SIR JOHN: Their money has been weighed, successfully, and has left London in a ship.

BARNARD: And how's a ship gonna gerrup the 'umber?

SIR JOHN: Oak, wind and floating devices.

BARNARD: The King's ship, The Providence, is in the estuary!

SIR JOHN: Sodom!

DURAND: The King's navy is in the Humber?

BARNARD: Packed wi' powder and troops from 'olland!

SIR JOHN: But how did it get there?!

BARNARD: Erk, wind, and floating devices!

SIR JOHN: If this is true why has Captain Moyer not informed me of this?

BARNARD: In haste, he's sailed out the 'arbour on The 'ercules and is engaging them now!

SIR JOHN: Lies! No, no, there is no King's navy. This is an invention, to pressure me to turn over to the King's side. Nothing but a masque –

Cannon fire is heard.

an elaborate masque with naval cannon sound effects.

More cannon fire.

how do I know you haven't rented that schooner?

BARNARD: You're all alone now Hotham.

SIR JOHN: *(Aside.)* The scales suddenly tip toward the royal party, like a see-saw with two evenly weighted children happily playing when suddenly an enormous ox falls out of a tree and lands on one end. What to do?! Am I a man, or am I two horses in double harness? Two horses pulling in opposite directions. The horse called "Honour" pulls towards Parliament; the horse called "Advantage" draws me to the King. Honour / Advantage. Honour / Advantage. Choose honour and I am disadvantaged. Choose Advantage and I am dishonoured. Honour / advantage / disadvantage / dishonour.

BARNARD: With events going agin yer I'll wager yer as ripe to roll over as a tuppeny whore.

SIR JOHN: I don't use tuppeny whores. Prudently, I save all my pennies and treat myself on Christmas Eve to –

DURAND: – he's calling you a cheap whore father!

BARNARD: All you care about is keeping your estates. Whoever wins the war.

DURAND: Not once, not twice, but thrice you besmirch my father's reputation!

BARNARD: Besmirch do I?

SIR JOHN: My honour has ne'er been so much such besmutched!

BARNARD: 'ull folk are direct. My truths, which you call insults, are the least of your worries. How yer gonna manage without an 'ead?

SIR JOHN: I shall adapt.

BARNARD: Yer can't educate pork!

> *BARNARD leaves passing a messenger in the doorway.*

SIR JOHN: Connie! What to do?

MESSENGER: You have mail!

FRANCES flies out of her room. She grabs letters but also gives letters.

FRANCES: A letter from James, but nothing from Rupert?

MESSENGER: How many followers do you have?

FRANCES: Two. James and Rupert.

MESSENGER: Rupert? Sorry, nothing.

MESSENGER exits.

FRANCES: *(In a negative swoon.)* Rupert has unfollowed me!

SIR JOHN: Come here you febrile doe! Give me that!

He tears the letter open and reads.

James. The Duke of York?! My fair lily…

She staggers around the room and then faints and rolls over the sofa, collapsing panting.

DURAND: James loves my sister? What does he say?

SIR JOHN: It's all acronyms, written in haste. C.U.L F.T.F. K.O.T.L.

CONNIE: See you later, face to face, kiss on the lips.

DURAND: He loves her!

SIR JOHN: Wait! If that sliver of quivering whimsy marries the Duke of York what would I be, to him?

DURAND: Father-in-Law.

SIR JOHN: And I would be the King's brother-in-law and the king would be my king-in-law, which should be enough to make him think twice about beheading me.

CONNIE: Stick that where the sun don't shine Black Tom.

DURAND: But by law and contract Frances is to marry Peregrine Pelham.

SIR JOHN: Argh! But we can't be allied to Parliament any longer! Not now, with the King's navy in the river.

He sinks to his knees in despair.

Connie? How do I give the town over to the King and yet –

CONNIE: – avoid the betrayal of Parliament?

DURAND: And the inevitable execution.

SIR JOHN: Yes!

CONNIE: Your first problem is the mob.

DURAND: Yes.

CONNIE: Pay them for the billeting or you will never see another day.

DURAND: Yes.

SIR JOHN: With Pelham's dowry from the strong box?

DURAND: No!

SIR JOHN: Why not?

DURAND: That is no longer our money. I like you a lot Father, but I love the law.

CONNIE: Borrow a thousand from the money lender.

SIR JOHN: Albert Calvert, the Jew?

ALL: He's not Jewish!

CONNIE: *(To DURAND.)* Get him over here. Tell him it's for the billeting.

DURAND: What shall I say has changed?

SIR JOHN: Tell him I have a secret that I had not previously disclosed.

> *DURAND leaves. SIR JOHN holds CONNIE, kisses the top of her head.*

Oh Connie if only you weren't low born I could be happy and want for nothing. But since you're a coarse peasant with no breeding, there's an end to that.

Knocking at the door. CONNIE opens the door to the DUKE OF YORK, dressed as a fishwife.

CONNIE: No hawkers or costers!

YORK elbows his way in.

Oi!

YORK: I am not a fish wife! I beg an audience. I am James, the Duke of York.

SIR JOHN: You're a man, are you? Prove it.

YORK: I shall not expose myself.

SIR JOHN: Reasonable.

SIR JOHN goes up and puts his hand under her skirts to check gender. This takes an inordinate amount of time, and searching, and consideration until –

SIR JOHN: Ah! Got it. *(Genuflects.)* Come in your majesty!

YORK: Good sir, your daughter!

He runs to her, moved that she might be dead.

SIR JOHN: She read your letter.

YORK: Is she not well?

SIR JOHN: She's as mad as a sack full of wet chickens. And would make a perfect wife. This is her daily swoon.

YORK: My father is a mercurial beast.

SIR JOHN: He declared me guilty of high treason!

YORK: Yes, but he'll return, and when he does, invite him in to inspect the arsenal, and I guarantee that he will relent, annul your death sentence, and treat you like family.

SIR JOHN: Like a brother-in-law?

YORK: Yes, and who would kill their brother?

SIR JOHN: Cain, Medea, Eteocles, Polyneices, Claudius, Romulus, –

YORK: – My father was not raised by wolves.

SIR JOHN: But my turning, away from Parliament, back to my only true calling, your father, must be a secret or Captain Moyer will clap me in irons.

YORK: The King will send an emissary.

YORK makes to leave.

A letter for your son, Durand.

SIR JOHN: He's not here.

SIR JOHN takes the letter, sniffs it.

YORK: From a lady admirer.

SIR JOHN: She's wasting her time, he has no interest in love.

YORK: Or girls?

SIR JOHN: On his fourteenth birthday I gave him a shilling, so he could have a whore, but he spent the money on a book about pigeons.

SIR JOHN gives YORK the letter back.

YORK: This girl is different. He might be interested in her.

YORK leaves.

SIR JOHN: Connie! We're now for the King! So, if the King returns how can I let him in and also bar him? I have to continue to bar him or Pelham will have Moyer clap me in irons.

CONNIE: How can a person be outside the walls and inside the walls at the same time?

SIR JOHN: Yes! Is that possible, or is it against nature?

CONNIE: It is only possible if the person is a king.

SIR JOHN: The king is a king!

CONNIE: When a person says "the King is coming", they don't mean a man on his own. No King travels alone. You can let the King in, but bar his attendants.

SIR JOHN: Connie, you're an ill bred, uncouth, plebeian, damned feculent miracle!

Enter DURAND and CALVERT.

SIR JOHN: *(In Hebrew rocks back and forth chanting the Shema.)*

Shema yisroel Adonai elohenu Adonai ehad

> *(For the second line he closes his eyes and presses his fingers to the lids.)*

Baruch Shem kavod Malchuto laolam vaed.

CALVERT: Are you Jewish?

SIR JOHN: Where there's smoke there's salmon.

CALVERT: Circumcised?

SIR JOHN: Abraham himself wasn't circumcised until he was ninety.

CALVERT: He did well then, getting to ninety without an interest free loan. What kind of Jew isn't cut?

SIR JOHN: We Berber Jews have dispensation from circumcision because the Atlas Mountains, where we live, are quite draughty, and you need all the layers you can get.

CALVERT: But then anyone could tell me they're a Berber Jew and get a discount.

SIR JOHN: Ah! So you do favour the old religion?

CALVERT: The only tribes I favour are those who repay. I'll lend you a thousand, interest free, because that is the only way I shall be paid my fourteen shillings for the billeting of troops. I'll draw up a contract.

SIR JOHN: Bring the money today!

CALVERT leaves.

Yes!

DURAND: I didn't know we were Jewish.

FRANCES wakes up with a start.

93

FRANCES: Yes! If I'm Jewish I can't marry Pelham!

SIR JOHN: We're not!

CONNIE: And neither is he.

SIR JOHN: I got the money didn't I! Here, a letter for you.

DURAND: For me?

SIR JOHN: From a lady.

DURAND: Does she need legal advice?

SIR JOHN: No, she needs something more enjoyable and less expensive.

> *He hands over the letter. DURAND takes it into his room.*

Connie! You may have saved my head!

> *He hugs and kisses her. Enter PELHAM at pace. He catches them in the act.*

PELHAM: Sir John! What – !?

SIR JOHN: She'd swallowed a key, accidentally, I was sucking it out.

> *He sticks his fingers down CONNIE's throat and comes up with a key, actually the key to the strong box.*

Be more careful next time you stupid mare!

> *CONNIE, takes the key.*

What is it Pelham?

PELHAM: The King!

SIR JOHN: *(Aside.)* My brother-in-law!

PELHAM: *(Aside.)* What did he say?

> *The King has returned, he's before the Beverley Gate. Haste man!*

> *PELHAM exits.*

END OF SCENE

SCENE TWO

The streets, inside the walls. Busy, soldiers, traders etc. YORK and
RUPERT are there with the fish stall. YORK is watching DURAND
promenade. RUPERT organises the fish stall.

RUPERT: Wir need parsley.

YORK: We're not here to sell fish Rupert.

RUPERT: Selbsverstendlich! Der fish stall ist ein Trojan Horse
for getting inside the arsenal!

YORK: Yes, and then I'd like to prove that statue of conceit
human, and restore love to its rightful place above the law
as the pinnacle of human achievement. He approaches! We
will find out.

RUPERT heads off. Enter DURAND.

Fresh sea bass sir!

DURAND: Your letter offered me truth, not fish.

YORK: I know a truth you don't know.

DURAND: You don't even know your fish. That's a cod.
Not a sea bass. Cod have beards, like men, see, it is an
unchanging variance of their species.

YORK: You're a man, and you don't have a beard.

DURAND: Because unlike a cod, victim to fate, I reason, I
cogitate, I change my destiny by shaving each morning.

YORK: To please a lady?

DURAND: To please no woman.

YORK: You don't like women?

DURAND: I shave to soothe my chin.

YORK: *(Aside.)* Greek!

Actually, my mistress is quite boyish.

DURAND: Tribadic?

YORK: She'll try anything once. She finds pleasure in the sight of your chin. Smooth, like a sea bass, unlike a cod. In fact the seabassnessness of your chin is the only conversation on this fish stall.

DURAND: I have no time for love, nor it for me. Truth is my only passion.

YORK: A shame for truth is abstract.

DURAND: Truth is tangible in the law, and fairer than any woman, and shall become more perfect with age through the incorporation of precedent, until it is, eventually, flawless.

YORK: The law is the custody, the safeguard of all private interests, liberty, property and honour, but what it can't do is hold you, kiss you, and transport you into raptures of bliss.

DURAND: By what name does your lady –

YORK: – Rupert..ia

DURAND: And is she pleasing on the eye?

YORK: Does that concern you?

DURAND: Not at all. I need the information to recognise her.

YORK: My mistress is not conventionally beautiful. She eschews fashion, believing it to be nothing more than socially approved construct.

DURAND: *(Aside.)* Tediously pedantic, like me!

She seems an exceptional intellect, for a fishmonger?

YORK: Ice was her idea.

DURAND: How does she like to pass the time?

YORK: She has a bookish interest in books.

DURAND: Building a library?

YORK: Specialising in semiotics and pigeons.

DURAND: *(Aside.)* Mine own two passions!

YORK: I have often heard her say that the word "modern" has no inherent meaning.

DURAND: It doesn't. Modern is –

YORK: – don't tell me, tell her.

> *RUPERT approaches.*

Here he is – she is now!

DURAND: Quickly. Give me a fish.

YORK: Two farthings.

> *DURAND is handed a fish. RUPERT approaches.*

DURAND: I have bought this fish.

RUPERT: Sehr Gut! Best before sunset.

DURAND: How *modern* is it?

RUPERT: It is frisch, fresh, very modern.

DURAND: But what does the word *modern* tell us about this fish?

RUPERT: Ich weiss nicht.

DURAND: You speak German, a language over four hundred years old, and yet we call it a *modern* European language. This fish, which is also modern, is not four hundred years old. The word modern contains no meaning, and only tells us that there were fish before this fish. I will keep it. As a bookmark.

> *He puts the fish in his book. YORK puts his arm through RUPERT's arm and hands DURAND a rose.*

DURAND: Fur mich?

RUPERT: Dich.

DURAND: Thank you, Rupertia. Danke.

> *DURAND walks off backwards.*

RUPERT: I think he likes me.

YORK: Yes, and now we must make a proper Malvolio of him.

YORK takes up a quill and writing paper and writes.

Clothing – yellow, a cod piece –

RUPERT: – a false nose!

YORK: Yes, he's already declared for noses!

Enter SIR JOHN. He is joined by DURAND and approached by BARNARD.

BARNARD: Good news! Hotham! The Earl of Newcastle has ridden south with most of the royalist gentry and is already at Wetwang, and with the King's navy in the 'umber, we will have our day soon enough. Keep yer word!

BARNARD skulks off. PELHAM approaches.

PELHAM: The King has returned. He is before the Beverley Gate with about fifty horse.

SIR JOHN: Any foot?

PELHAM: None brother.

SIR JOHN: Fifty horse and no feet?!

PELHAM: Your orders from Parliament require you to bar him.

SIR JOHN: A second time. He's behaving like Hull was his favourite pub.

Enter a soldier running.

SOLDIER: They got the King on a ladder sir!

The King appears atop a ladder overlooking the walls. Soldiers take aim.

SIR JOHN: Hold fire! Let me reason with him!

Fanfare.

CHARLES: Hotham! An opportunity, to make amends to your earlier affront.

SIR JOHN: Your majesty, I have never said you can't come in. Only your troop, your horse, your foot cannot enter.

PELHAM: Remember your orders Hotham!

CHARLES: So a King is invited to enter this nest of rebels *alone*?! I will need at least thirty attendants for security.

SIR JOHN: Six.

CHARLES: Twenty-five!

SIR JOHN: Fourteen! That's my final offer. Fourteen is already thrice six!

CHARLES: I shall not reprise King Lear! Harassed from daughter to daughter, begging a meal!

SIR JOHN: What's he talking about?

SOLDIER 1: King Lear. Shakespeare's old King.

SIR JOHN: I don't know it. What happens?

SOLDIER 2: The King goes mad and dies.

SIR JOHN: Is that it?

SOLDIER 1: Yes.

SIR JOHN: Three and a half hours?

SOLDIER 2: And the rest.

SIR JOHN: Your majesty, we do not wish you to go mad and die. You are our King, and welcome in Hull, alone. I have prepared a bed chamber for you in my house.

CHARLES: You pile indignity on affront! This disobedience of yours will cause much loss of blood, which could be avoided if you perform your duty as a subject. War is inevitable now, and on your conscience!

> *CHARLES is lowered out of sight. The Parliament troops heckle and chant.*

SOLDIERS: War! War! War!

END OF SCENE

The RANTER sings.

A SONG OF WAR

THE FAMILISTS ARE RECRUITING, THE LEVELLERS FALL IN
THE ROUNDHEADS ARE PREPARING, THE WAR WILL SOON BEGIN.
THE ROYALISTS, MAY KNOCK US DOWN, THEY WON'T EXPECT IT
WHEN
THE PEOPLE OF HULL RISE UP AND THEN THEY RISE UP ONCE
AGAIN.

LET'S SING A SONG OF WAR.
FATHERS, BROTHERS, SONS.
LET'S SING A SONG OF WAR.
GET YOUR MUSKETS, PIKES AND DRUMS.
LET'S SING A SONG OF WAR.
A SONG FOR EVERYONE.

THE REBELLION WILL RISE UP, SIZE UP THE ENEMY.
THEY'LL HEAR THE DREADFUL CRIES "UP WITH PARLIAMENT AND
HULL".
SO BROTHERS COME AND SIGN UP, LINE UP THE ENEMY
STRAIGHTEN YOUR SPINE UP, AND PRAY FOR A MIRACLE.

LET'S SING A SONG OF WAR.
FATHERS, BROTHERS, SONS.
(THE REBELLION WILL RISE UP, SIZE UP THE ENEMY.)
LET'S SING A SONG OF WAR.
GET YOUR MUSKETS, PIKES AND DRUMS.
(THEY'LL HEAR THE DREADFUL CRIES "UP WITH PARLIAMENT AND
HULL".)
LET'S SING A SONG OF WAR.
A WAR FOR EVERYONE.
(BROTHERS COME AND SIGN UP, LINE UP THE ENEMY.)
A WAR FOR EVERYONE.
(BROTHERS COME AND SIGN UP, LINE UP THE ENEMY.)
A WAR FOR EVERYONE.

Act Five

The house. Enter SARAH and SALTMARSH from the street. SARAH has two hat boxes.

SARAH: There is no one in. My husband is currently charming the King.

SALTMARSH: But we must be swift! If he is arrested, all your goods will be confiscated and the money commandeered. Where's Pelham's dowry?

SARAH: Secure in a strong box in the bedroom. This newly minted key is not tested.

SALTMARSH: Not the bedroom with the Inigo Jones bed?

SARAH: Yes. But you must not look at …oh sod it, come this way I'd like to show you the bed.

They go into the bedroom.

SALTMARSH: *(Off.)* Oh my God!

SARAH: *(Off.)* Not now Parsnip!

SARAH comes out running, with SALTMARSH after, who grabs her and kisses her. Enter DRUDGE from the street carrying the vase like a baby.

SARAH: Drudge? What's happening?

DRUDGE mimes that it's all over and that SIR JOHN is coming back.

SARAH: He's coming back! Quick! Get in the coal cellar.

She opens the hatch and SALTMARSH goes down into the cellar. Enter SIR JOHN, DURAND, FRANCES, and CONNIE.

SIR JOHN: Drudge put that damn vase down.

DRUDGE draws a knife.

Give me the knife!? Or you're going on the hook!

CONNIE: He doesn't have a hook here.

SIR JOHN: The knife or I'll put up a hook!

CONNIE goes down into the cellar, but shouts up.

CONNIE: *(Off.)* Who are you!?

SIR JOHN: Who is it Connie?

SALTMARSH: *(Off.)* I am Sir John's cousin.

SIR JOHN: A cousin? Ask him if he's the mad one from Heslerton?

CONNIE: *(Off.)* Are you the mad one from Heslerton?

SALTMARSH: *(Off.)* Yes.

SIR JOHN: Let him up.

SALTMARSH appears, CONNIE after.

If you needed coal Mister Saltmarsh just ask? But I would have thought seventeen wives was enough to keep a man warm.

SALTMARSH: That is not how the Family of Love works.

SIR JOHN: I want you to stop using your cant to excite the people.

SALTMARSH: It was a different kind of cant that closed the gates on the King.

SIR JOHN: I was commissioned by Parliament.

SALTMARSH: Parliament is just another emperor, but by another name.

SIR JOHN: And what name is that?

SALTMARSH: Parliament.

SIR JOHN: You're a gentleman, you have the vote.

SALTMARSH: Which I will never use until every Englishman is so entitled. Parliament is the gentry legitimising their illegitimate powers.

SARAH: He has renounced his birthright.

SIR JOHN: What an idiot.

SALTMARSH: I have chosen to be a wretch.

SIR JOHN: You would have every man, regardless of his station, given the vote?

SALTMARSH: And every woman.

SIR JOHN: *(Spits out his drink.)* You would give my wife the vote?

SALTMARSH: Why not your wife sir?

SIR JOHN: Because a compendious knowledge of shoes and sitting down to piss does not qualify one to elect a national assembly!

SALTMARSH: *(Re CONNIE.)* And this woman.

SIR JOHN: She's a servant?!

SALTMARSH: Master and Servant has no grounding in the New Testament.

SIR JOHN: *(Re CONNIE.)* Conceived in a ditch!? Out of wedlock. Quickly, without poetry or payment. A hedgehog has a finer pedigree!

SALTMARSH: She seems to me a credit to God. With a fine wit.

SIR JOHN: No learning! No land! No money! What would she vote for?

CONNIE: Learning, land and money.

SIR JOHN: No! *My* learning, my land and my money!

SALTMARSH: Why, if you have "all your land", should she not have "all your land"?

SIR JOHN: You would have us all levelled?!

SALTMARSH: At one time this woman owned England.

SIR JOHN: Sceptical nonsense!

SALTMARSH: She owned the land in common with others, before it was stolen from her by enclosure.

CONNIE: Middleton-on-the-Wolds actually.

SIR JOHN: Enclosure was not theft!

DURAND: It was an issue of Parliament.

CONNIE: In which, without the vote, my father could not participate.

SIR JOHN: Oh, not you Connie. Not you, you're all –

SALTMARSH: – why should one man have four thousand pounds a year and another exist on but a single pound?

SIR JOHN: Because I am Sir John Hotham! A Hotham! A damned feculent gentleman, from an unbroken line dating back to the eleventh century. Get out! This is enough revolution for one lifetime. Out! *(To SARAH.)* Go with him if you must!

> *SALTMARSH and SARAH leave. The door closes. A knock. CONNIE opens it. A MESSENGER is there with letters. FRANCES devours the letters and gives some back then runs back up to her room. Then she realises that one of the letters is for DURAND, and gives it on. DURAND gives the MESSENGER a letter. This is all done amazingly swiftly.*

SIR JOHN: Like the twitter of birds.

> *DURAND takes it and retires to his room, but only after giving the messenger a letter.*

SIR JOHN: *(To CONNIE.)* Forgive me.

CONNIE: The hedgehog bit?

SIR JOHN: Yes.

CONNIE: Money did change hands.

SIR JOHN: Ah. You said your mother was enterprising.

CONNIE: Cherub, you're troubled?

SIR JOHN: My lunatic cousin has confirmed my worst fears.

CONNIE: The mob?

SIR JOHN: What might the people want if they begin to imagine? A lowly smith, a carter, a glover, might fancy himself my equal. Forget Parliament or King, if the mob act they could level the rich of both parties.

> *Knocking on the door. CONNIE opens it, MOYER and FROTTAGE enter.*

MOYER: Sir, events sir, events!

SIR JOHN: *(Looking at FROTTAGE.)* This is the event Captain Moyer!

MOYER: My ship The Hercules engaged with the royalist schooner in the Humber –

SIR JOHN: – schooner? You mean the King's navy?

MOYER: One ship sir, which fled, running aground near Paull.

SIR JOHN: Who's Paul?

MOYER: Paull is the name of a small village up a creek east of here.

SIR JOHN: Damn stupid name for a village up a creek.

MOYER: The Cavaliers fled on foot, and my crew took their marines prisoner.

SIR JOHN: *(Aside.)* The painful wind of history has blown and an elephant has landed on the Parliament end of the see-saw. The see-saw, has see-sawed back again, which is why they're called see-saws, back to favour Parliament. And I am stuck in the middle, not knowing which end of the see-saw to ride, like a man with two horses but only one arse. But she's a loin exciter. *(To MOYER.)* And is this the Royalist captain?

MOYER: This sir is a lady.

SIR JOHN: I can see that Captain Moyer.

MOYER: Aristocracy, and French.

FROTTAGE: Parlez vous Francais?

SIR JOHN: Oui! Wilkommen!

MOYER: She is Queen Henrietta's lady of the bedchamber.

FROTTAGE: Enchanté.

SIR JOHN: J'arrive!

MOYER: She gives her name as Madame Félicité de Frottage D'Aquitaine. She is a prisoner –

SIR JOHN: – une guest d'honneur.

SIR JOHN kisses her hand.

MOYER: The other prisoners are secure in irons in the fo'c'sle but she, being a lady and so fair, I didn't know …could you iron her here?

CONNIE: *(Aside.)* To iron. Verb. To clap in irons.

SIR JOHN: Pro bono. She shall have the Inigo Jones bed, in the King's room.

MOYER: But I thought your wife was in there sir?

SIR JOHN: She was.

SOLDIER: Sir…!

MOYER: I must return to the walls. The papists are camped only a mile off.

SIR JOHN: Our King is hardly a Papist Captain Moyer.

MOYER: His Queen is. Or do you soften sir?

SIR JOHN: Soft?! Moi!? Non! J'ai bois!

MOYER: Good! After today's display of defiance the company and I are much emboldened. Let this war begin! And in Hull!

SIR JOHN: Au revoir! Mon brave!

MOYER exits. SIR JOHN closes the door and considers his new adventure.

(Re FROTTAGE, to himself.) Once more into the breach.

FROTTAGE: Monsieur?

SIR JOHN: Encore une fois! Entrer nous dedans la breach. Cest une famoose Anglaisy speechy Monsieur William Shakespeare.

FROTTAGE: Qui?

SIR JOHN: I have the keys to all the rooms. The master suite is your prison cell, with a bed designed by Inigo Jones.

FROTTAGE: Inigo Jones the libertine?

SIR JOHN: I presumed he was a bed designer. If you look at the bed, you will be conquered.

FROTTAGE: The mere sight of the bed fires the passions?

SIR JOHN: They can't use straw for the mattress. They use duck down from non-flammable ducks. You're speaking English?

FROTTAGE: *(Whisper.)* I am not Madame Frottage. That was a part I played for Captain Moyer. *(Re CONNIE and DRUDGE.)* The servants.

SIR JOHN: Connie, Drudge, leave us alone!

CONNIE: *(Aside.)* How many times have I seen this moment? His passion lasts, a year, two years, and then one day he'll seek me out, and at length he'll describe the witch he fell in love with, and beg some comfort, which I give him, for he is all I have.

CONNIE exits into the coal cellar.

FROTTAGE: I am Lady Digby, of the King's court, a messenger.

SIR JOHN: But if someone finds me talking to a member of the royal party –

FROTTAGE: – I entreat you, reconsider your position vis a vis the King.

SIR JOHN: You're speaking French again?!

FROTTAGE: Hand over the arsenal and you will regain his favour.

SIR JOHN: No! Ten minutes ago he had a ship in the Humber and looked like taking the town, then he lost that ship. And now Parliament again prevails and anyway the King declared me a traitor!

FROTTAGE: Give him the munitions and he will pardon you.

SIR JOHN: As well as not beheading me, would he give me a baronetcy?

FROTTAGE: You're already a baron.

SIR JOHN: I've always wanted to be a double baron.

FROTTAGE: He will let you keep your head, is that not enough?

SIR JOHN: Lady Digby, how can I?! Parliament is in the ascendant. It would be suicide for me. But I will not betray you to Captain Moyer, you must stay the night.

FROTTAGE: No, get me a horse, I shall ride to the King.

SIR JOHN: No! You haven't seen the bed yet. And anyway, it's Holy Horse Day today.

FROTTAGE: A holiday for horses?

SIR JOHN: A Hull tradition. Once a year they can wear what they like; eat pancakes; and shit in the road. Let me show you the room that the bed's in, the one you can't look at.

> *SIR JOHN opens the door and she goes in and he is about to follow when DURAND opens his door, and comes out. SIR JOHN slams his door. DURAND is now dressed in a yellow costume decorated with roses, a cod piece, and a huge nose.*

SIR JOHN: What the feculent hell is that?!

DURAND: – Pater. Tis I.

SIR JOHN: You look like a daffodil with the horn. Two horns!

DURAND: I am an object of desire.

SIR JOHN: A woman?

DURAND: Possibly.

SIR JOHN: But why dress like that?

DURAND: To please her.

SIR JOHN: From which end.

DURAND: She is enchanted by my chin but finds my nose disappointing.

SIR JOHN: But who built it, it must've taken weeks?

DURAND: I made it out of pig skin and stuck it on with fish glue. I never knew before the ecstasy of purposeful suffering.

There is banging on the door and BARNARD enters.

SIR JOHN: You can't just come –

BARNARD: – Refuge! The mob besiege mi 'ouse! Why don't yer pay them!

SIR JOHN: I shall send you the money today. Before dinner.

BARNARD: I don't trust you Hotham.

BARNARD sees DURAND.

Bugger me! I'll 'ave to tek mi socks off!

SIR JOHN: My son. He's in love.

BARNARD: Oh that explains it then.

DURAND: Do you doubt my father's word!?

BARNARD: I doubt bloody everything about him! I doubt he is standing here before me! I have never in my entire puff met such… doubling duplicity, such a pestiferous purpose changer, such Janus faced Pharasaical frontage!

SIR JOHN: And I'm glad that in insulting me you have at last found full employment for your limited education! I demand you leave!

There's beating on the door.

BARNARD: Refuge!

SIR JOHN: The cellar.

BARNARD goes down into the cellar. CONNIE comes straight out.

CONNIE: This is my coal cellar and I in't sharing it wi' no one! Who's that banging on the door!

SIR JOHN: Don't open –

CONNIE opens the door and lets in CALVERT.

SIR JOHN: Shalom Aleichem!

CALVERT: I have the contract for your loan. With an additional clause. Since you are indebted to me now in blood.

He produces a written legal contract.

DURAND: Blood?

CALVERT: A clown Hotham?

SIR JOHN: My son, he's in love.

CALVERT: Oh, bad luck. Blood because my daughter has been tupped, and her maidenhead taken.

SIR JOHN: I am neither taker nor tupper. I've been too busy, and in here.

CALVERT: I know the ram! He is a Parliament soldier, quartered for nowt in my house, having no diversions but porter, wine and the horn, and now I contract for an equivalent injury from you!

SIR JOHN: You're Hull's Shylock eh? You want a pound of flesh?

CALVERT: An ounce.

> *He gives* SIR JOHN *the contract,* SIR JOHN *gives it to* DURAND.

DURAND: The party of the first part –

CALVERT: – that's me.

DURAND: – agrees to loan a thousand pounds to the party of the second part –

SIR JOHN: – is that me?

CALVERT: Yes, you.

DURAND: As surety the party of the second part –

SIR JOHN: Me.

DURAND: – provides his foreskin.

SIR JOHN: My foreskin?

CALVERT: Your foreskin.

SIR JOHN: My foreskin?

CALVERT: Your foreskin.

SIR JOHN: *(Re DURAND.)* Would his foreskin suffice?

CALVERT: No. I want yours.

SIR JOHN: It's the only one I have, and I use it a lot!

CALVERT: I can only lend this money interest free to a Jew.

DURAND: But you're not Jewish.

CALVERT: I am a free man and can make my own terms. My daughter has been violated. An eye for an eye. A tooth for a tooth.

SIR JOHN: You can have a tooth. Two teeth? Three teeth, one eye, and a finger! And that's my last offer.

CALVERT: Whenever you need it, the money's here?

> *CALVERT is gone. Enter CAPTAIN MOYER.*

MOYER: We are alone Sir John.

SIR JOHN: No, no! My son is here.

MOYER: Alone in Yorkshire. Fairfax will not fight.

The hounds bark, go crazy, and just as quickly stop.

DURAND: Fairfax?

The hounds bark, go crazy, and just as quickly stop.

SIR JOHN: Which feculent son of a bachelor thought it was a good idea to bring a pack of hounds to Hull?!

Beat.

Can't a man make one mistake!?

DURAND: With regard to Black Tom... what is the detail?

MOYER: He shall not raise a pike against his King.

DURAND: He has signed a deed of neutrality?

MOYER: And the Queen has landed at Bridlington with a Dutch army. Do you have orders for me Sir?

SIR JOHN: Yes. Cancel all leave.

MOYER goes to leave.

MOYER: Is Madame Frottage –

SIR JOHN: Don't worry about her, I'll sort her out later.

SIR JOHN: *(Aside.)* An enormous blue whale falls out of the tree and lands on the see-saw slinging Parliament's elephant into the Humber. Victory for the King is inevitable. Thank God we have Lady Digby!

A MESSENGER with letters enters, passing MOYER in the doorway. FRANCES comes out of her room, collects her letters from the MESSENGER and gives him further letters. FRANCES sits and reads the latest letter. This business is ignored by the others. SARAH enters from the street.

SIR JOHN: What's my cousin offered you? Wife number eighteen?

SARAH: Equivalence. Rights. Respect.

SIR JOHN: Would you be free of me!? A divorce?

SARAH: No. I would profit more from your death, and the Hull mob might have that intent. My wit tells me to wait. *(To DURAND.)* In love?

DURAND: Yes, mater.

SARAH: Is it a girl?

DURAND: I'm not sure.

FROTTAGE: *(Off.)* Monsieur Hotham?! Que se passe-t-il?

SARAH: Why is there a French woman in the bedroom?

SIR JOHN: It's Holy Horse day. The horses get the day off, and you have to lock a French woman in the bedroom. Or it's six years' bad luck.

> *FROTTAGE emerges from the bedroom.*

SARAH: Where did he find you?

FROTTAGE: *(To SARAH.)* Je suis Madame Félicité de Frottage.

SARAH: Lady congratulations of rubbing?

FROTTAGE: – D'Aquitaine.

SARAH: Of water sports.

FROTTAGE: Je suis la dame de la chambre de lit de la Reine Henrietta.

SARAH: And my arse is the temple of Venus.

SIR JOHN: She is an emissary from the King himself.

SARAH: So you're the King's tart!? You're not French!

SIR JOHN: She's masking a French lady, to fool Captain Moyer.

SARAH: Connie! What is happening here?!

CONNIE: The Dutch are coming, Black Tom is not coming, and Newcastle's arrived. Now it would be wise to surrender Hull to the King.

SARAH: Why ?

SIR JOHN: Don't you want to end the war on the winning side ?!

CONNIE: *(To FROTTAGE.)* Will the King renounce the *traitor condemnation* if Sir John surrenders?

FROTTAGE: That is already agreed.

SIR JOHN: I can't surrender just like that, Captain Moyer would clap me in irons.

CONNIE: *(To LADY DIGBY.)* Arrange for the King to advance, in large numbers, to surround the town –

MOB: – city!

CONNIE: – and to make a show of firing on the arsenal –

SIR JOHN: – but if the stores are hit we will all be blown to hell!

CONNIE: Which is why I said "make a show of".

FROTTAGE: So the King fires once aiming to miss, and not at the arsenal.

CONNIE: *(To SIR JOHN.)* Then you, aware that one stray incendiary could fire the powder and kill every soul in Hull, you surrender the city to protect the innocent citizens –

SIR JOHN: – who see the wisdom in my decision and might then decide not to tear me limb from limb –

CONNIE: – because you'd saved them.

SIR JOHN: Connie, my sweet, if only you weren't a woman you might have made something of yourself.

Mob banging on the doors.

DURAND: The mob again Father. We don't have the money to pay them off! And I'm not getting circumcised.

CONNIE: Mister Pelham's dowry, the two thousand is in the strongbox in the bedroom.

CONNIE produces the key.

SARAH: What's she doing with the key?

SIR JOHN: Don't you trust her?

SARAH: No!

CONNIE gives the key to SIR JOHN.

DURAND: The money may be in our house, but it's not ours. Pelham took possession, signed a contract, it's his money, unless legally challenged.

SIR JOHN: Legally challenged?

CONNIE: Or exposed as an adulterer, with another woman in the Inigo Jones bed, with my lady.

CONNIE looks to SARAH.

SARAH: You impudent strumpet!

SIR JOHN: This might work! Pelham is more enamoured of you than Frances.

SARAH: I will not –

SIR JOHN: – Shutup, you eviscerated gold truffling sow.

SARAH: Durand? Is this the law?

DURAND: In common law a betrothal contract is annulled if either party is witnessed *in flagrante delicto* with another.

CONNIE: You invite Pelham into the bedroom, with that bed –

SARAH: – I'm not playing the lead in this masque for no reward.

SIR JOHN: *(To SARAH.)* Divorce, and two thousand a year.

SARAH: Where would I live?

SIR JOHN: And a house.

SARAH looks unmoved.

Two houses. Three houses!? Alright! Bridlington!?

SARAH: Agreed! Does it have to be *in flagrante delicto*? Or can it be just *in flagrante*?

DURAND: The witnesses must consider Mr Pelham's intent to be obvious, let me explain –

SARAH: – I know what you mean.

SIR JOHN: Lady Digby you have saved England! Ride to the King tell him of our scheme and Hull is his! Drudge, saddle a horse!

FROTTAGE: But I thought it was Holy Horse Day?

SIR JOHN: For Christian horses it is, but we keep a Hindu mare well disposed for emergencies.

CONNIE: Avoid the mob, use the coal chute!

> *DRUDGE exits down the hatch with LADY DIGBY. SIR JOHN shouts down the hatch.*

SIR JOHN: Lord Mayor. This lady is an agent of the King. I'm handing him the town.

BARNARD: *(Off.)* Good lad!

CONNIE: *(To DURAND.)* How many witnesses d'yer need for proving adultery?

DURAND: Five gentlemen or twenty-seven yeomen.

SIR JOHN: Five gentlemen?! Where are we going to find five gentlemen in Hull!?

SARAH: Lord Mayor Barnard, that's one –

FRANCES: – the princes! Yes, the princes! Father please!

SIR JOHN: Two princes! So, two plus one, that's our five!

SARAH: – three!

DURAND: Mr Calvert, the money lender.

SIR JOHN: The Jew!?

ALL: He's not Jewish!

DURAND: He is a man of property, which makes him a gentleman.

SIR JOHN: Fetch him here!

DURAND exits.

SARAH: That's four.

SIR JOHN: My cousin, your lover, Saltmarsh.

SARAH: We are quorate!

SIR JOHN: Connie! We need to tempt Pelham here. Tell him that now is a good time for him to collect his money, as my wife has the key to the strong box.

SIR JOHN produces the key. Looks for SARAH.

Where has the damned feculent Sapphist gone?

SARAH: I'm here.

SIR JOHN: Darling. Take this key and we need something of you to tempt him, something redolent of you. Maybe an old shoe.

SARAH: He likes my hands. This glove will fire him.

SARAH gives CONNIE a glove. CONNIE leaves by the cellar.

SIR JOHN: *(To SARAH.)* Bring my cousin here. He will profit from this.

SARAH leaves.

SIR JOHN: Mister Barnard! Come up here please sir!

BARNARD comes up.

Sir, I am cuckolded by Mr Pelham. I need you to witness the Puritan's ardour.

BARNARD: What am I looking for?

SIR JOHN: It's not called ardour for nothing is it?

FRANCES: Shall I bring the princes? I am meeting James at four.

SIR JOHN: Which is now.

FRANCES: But I intend being late, it will heighten his desire, this is the theory according to poetry.

SIR JOHN: No, no, no. Now!

FRANCES leaves.

Come! To the bedroom!

END OF SCENE

Song – LO! THE BED!

LO! THE BED!

BEHOLD!
THE BED!

THE INIGO JONES BED!

AVERT YOUR EYES
AVERT YOUR EYES

LEST YOU BE TEMPTED BY... THE BED!

THE BED!
 THE BED!
 THE BED!

LO! THE BED!

SCENE TWO

The bedroom. A fabulous bed with a chandelier over. There are curtains, some oak panelling, a commode, and curtains. A series of strong boxes built into the panel wall.

SIR JOHN: *(To the audience.)* Don't look at the bed! I said, don't look at the bed! Right now, bugger off all of you... *Etc*

CHERUB: Wanker!

BARNARD: Where do I hide?

SIR JOHN: Under the bed!

> *MR BARNARD crawls under the bed. Enter SALTMARSH and SARAH.*

Cousin. We need to hide you somewhere. Under the bed with the Lord Mayor.

> *SALTMARSH goes under the bed. Enter MR CALVERT and DURAND.*

CALVERT: What is it Hotham? I am dragged through the streets of Hull, the mob following and –

SIR JOHN: You are here, as a gentleman, to witness Mr Pelham's ardour.

CALVERT: It will be a pleasure, I loathe the man.

SIR JOHN: Behind the curtains!

> *CALVERT goes behind the curtains. Enter DRUDGE with vase.*

Drudge! Get out! Get out! You can't watch!

> *DRUDGE refuses to leave. Enter FRANCES with the DUKE OF YORK and PRINCE RUPERT, both still in women's attire.*

SIR JOHN: Ah, my daughter! With her friends!

> *DURAND struts across. Offering a rose. He kneels before RUPERT.*

DURAND: As Adonis was mortal and Aphrodite a goddess, I supplicate myself before your deity, and requite your rose. I renounce the law and am committed to employ all my learning in the art of love, ars amandi, ars amatoria, or if my advances do not please you, ars moriendi. I implore you, leave your home even if it be heaven and come and live in Hull.

BARNARD: It is a cultured city.

CALVERT: There's a fast route to Holland and cheap tobacco.

SIR JOHN: You will not be inconvenienced by hills.

SARAH: It's only twelve hours to Bridlington.

CONNIE: Pelham's in the lobby!

SIR JOHN: Princes, find a place.

> *FRANCES grabs YORK and drags him behind a curtain. DURAND advances on RUPERT and they kiss. Everyone watches. Enter CONNIE.*
>
> *SARAH dramatically throws off her shawl.*

SIR JOHN: Bring him in!

CONNIE: Where will you hide?

SIR JOHN: Where else is there?

CONNIE: The commode!

> *SIR JOHN takes the pan out the back of the commode and hides in the back.*

CONNIE: Madam?

SARAH: I'm ready.

> *CONNIE exits. SIR JOHN pops up through the hole in the commode.*

SIR JOHN: Lay across the bed! You top heavy spleen farm! Show him the key!

DRUDGE puts the vase on a side table and climbs on to the chandelier, and lies there.

Drudge! Come down from there, you're not a gentleman, you can't watch!

Enter CONNIE, with PELHAM, averting his eyes from the bed.

CONNIE: Ma'am. Mr Peregrine Pelham, come to collect his money.

SARAH: Mr Pelham! Come through.

PELHAM: Good day Lady Hotham.

SARAH: Thank you Connie. Tell me, where is Sir John?

CONNIE: He's inspecting the Myton Gate block house.

SARAH: Did he say how long he would be?

CONNIE: About two hours ma'am, and if he returns unexpectedly I'll –

SARAH: – that's enough, thank you.

CONNIE exits.

You can look at the bed Mr. Pelham.

PELHAM: No! I'll just take my money. I shall not be tempted! For if I look I will fall victim to mine own febrile concupiscence.

SIR JOHN pops up and encourages SARAH, and in doing so, creeps the commode forward.

SARAH: Did you return my glove?

PELHAM: I have kept it here, in my breast pocket, next to my heart.

SARAH: Have you held it?

PELHAM: I touched it, yes.

SARAH: What did it feel like?

PELHAM: Inviting.

SARAH: It's goat skin.

PELHAM: It feels softer than that. I should know I touch a lot of goats.

SARAH: They soak the hide in cold urine.

PELHAM: Cold urine?

SIR JOHN pops up and suggests that she stop talking about urine.

SARAH: Yes, cold urine softens the skin, then they rub it until all the coarse hairs fall out, after which they stretch the hide over tenterhooks.

PELHAM: You seem to know a lot about it.

SARAH: I wanted to know what they were doing with my urine. Did you try the glove on?

PELHAM: I did.

SARAH: But you're a big man, with big hands.

PELHAM: I am!

SARAH: It must have been tight?

PELHAM: Yes! It felt like I was entering a small goat.

SARAH: That had been soaked in cold urine.

SIR JOHN pops up again protesting.

SARAH: If you feel the call of nature there is a commode over there.

PELHAM: I dearly would like to but I fear my current mettle will not allow it.

SIR JOHN pops his head out watching. CALVERT's head appears from behind the curtains.

CALVERT: *(Whispered.)* Ardour?

SIR JOHN: *(Whispered.)* It needs to be harder than that.

Some of the witnesses peep.

SARAH: Would a drink of cold water help?

> *SIR JOHN pops up threateningly, he's on to her game. This time he stands and lifts the commode off the floor and walks a couple of paces to one side to get a better view.*

SARAH: Throw the glove on the bed Mr Pelham.

PELHAM: I cannot look at the bed or I shall be destroyed!

SARAH: Do as I say.

> *PELHAM turns, holding the glove, and now he looks at the bed. The sight of the bed takes his breath away and gives him an erection.*

SARAH: It's an empty stage, awaiting the players.

PELHAM: An elixir for the imagination.

SARAH: And who do you see on the bed?

PELHAM: Lady Hotham.

SARAH: Frances, the young lady Hotham of your engagement, or –

PELHAM: – No! Please, not that fatuous, empty youth.

> *FRANCES comes out of hiding but is dragged back in by YORK.*

FRANCES: Oi –

SARAH: – oi, oi, oi.

> *SARAH undoes her stays dramatically. PELHAM rips his shirt off, buttons flying. The sound of love making coming from behind the curtains. SARAH coughs to cover it. SIR JOHN pops up questioningly.*

PELHAM: I hear love making! And that commode has moved!

SARAH: It is the effect of the bed. A fevered imagination infusing all the senses.

PELHAM: This house has a ghost.

SARAH: Yes, the ghost.

> *SARAH intercepts him and throws her arms around him, they kiss and fall heavily on to the bed. The bed visibly bends down under the weight and we hear a cry from BARNARD as the springs dig into him.*

BARNARD: 'kinnel!

PELHAM: I heard the cry of a man.

SARAH: That was me, my voice deepens when I yearn.

> *(In a deep voice.)* Argh! Oohhh! 'kinnel! Don't stop!

> *At that moment CAPTAIN JACK bursts in from down stage left. He is wearing the full uniform of a Roundhead, sword and scabbard and musket. PELHAM hides under the sheets.*

JACK: Step mother!

SARAH: Jack!

JACK: Are you safe? The mob are at the windows!

> *JACK throws his sword and scabbard off, and his cloak.*

They wouldn't let me pass, I had to climb in through one of the lights.

SARAH: They intend to take their money.

JACK: I have ridden hard from Beverley, two hours, not even stopping for nature. Mother! I need your commode!

SARAH: Yes! Over there!

JACK: I shall sit to spare your blushes!

> *He sits on the commode, urinates and vocalises his relief.*

Ooooh!

SIR JOHN: *(Muffled.)* Agh!

> *Urine runs out from the bottom of the commode. JACK has spotted DRUDGE and leaps off and draws his sword.*

JACK: Drudge! You peep on my mother in her chamber?!

SIR JOHN pushes his head through the hole, still unseen by JACK. DRUDGE falls on to the bed. The bed collapses flat down so that we fear for the lives of the gentlemen underneath. SARAH leaps up in the mayhem and goes to the strong boxes with the key. Plaintive groaning and wailing from BARNARD. SIR JOHN runs forward to JACK, still trapped in the commode and wet head sticking through the hole.

SIR JOHN: Jack! Sheath your sword!

JACK: Father, why are you wearing a commode?!

SIR JOHN: To unearth this fox!

JACK: What fox!?

Having no arms available since they're trapped in the commode. JACK throws back the sheets on PELHAM.

JACK: Father! You are cuckolded!

PELHAM tries to escape but JACK has his sword and swiftly bars his way to the door. SARAH has the money bags from the strong box. SIR JOHN runs around still trapped in the commode and tries to raise witnesses.

SIR JOHN: Mr Calvert! Witness this! Show yourself!

CALVERT shows himself.

Mr Calvert open the curtains, I have no hands!

CALVERT opens the curtains to reveal YORK and FRANCES fucking. SIR JOHN goes to the other curtains.

And this.

CALVERT opens that and witnesses DURAND and RUPERT fucking.

SIR JOHN: MR PELHAM! You are betrothed to my daughter and the bride price is paid! And yet you consort with my wife in her chamber! I declare the engagement nul and void, and require you to return the dowry forthwith.

PELHAM: Your word alone is not enough.

SIR JOHN: I have five witnesses to this perfidy! Mr. Calvert, his majesty the Duke of York, Prince Rupert.

PELHAM: Your numbers fail you once again Hotham.

SIR JOHN: Barnard and Saltmarsh are under the bed.

> *SIR JOHN looks down at a trickle of blood coming from under the bed.*

PELHAM: They may not live.

SIR JOHN: Lift the bed!

> *CALVERT, DURAND, YORK, and RUPERT lift the bed and BARNARD and SALTMARSH crawl out. BARNARD is covered in blood, but SALTMARSH is alright.*

SIR JOHN: The Lord Mayor of Hull, and my fifth witness, another landed gentleman, is John Saltmarsh.

PELHAM: Then I am undone. I confess, I was in thrall to my lust, and I shall return home and flagellate myself as is God's want.

> *PELHAM takes a leather belt and starts flagellating himself as he leaves. SARAH throws the money bags to SALTMARSH, who escapes.*

SIR JOHN: Vixen! The money! My cousin! You have schemed against me!

SARAH: You should have divorced me when you had the chance.

> *SARAH runs past him, he chases her and hits the door frame at pace. But he can't get through the door because of the width of the commode.*

SIR JACK: Who will rid me of this turbulent commode?! Jack! Stop her!

JACK: Who!

SIR JOHN: My wife! She's taken the money we need to appease the mob!

> *JACK chases after SARAH and SALTMARSH. BARNARD and*
> *CALVERT pull the commode off SIR JOHN. DURAND and*
> *RUPERT step back into the curtains kissing. Enter CONNIE.*

Where's your lady?!

CONNIE: She left the house.

SIR JOHN: How can she?! The mob's breaking in!

CONNIE: Through the coal chute.

> *Enter JACK at a pace.*

JACK: They've broken through a skylight. We must barricade
ourselves in!

SIR JOHN: Secure the door!

> *JACK, BARNARD and DRUDGE secure the door. We hear*
> *the mob at the bedroom door, and see the door flex from the*
> *pressure.*

BARNARD: What we gonna do? Hotham! You have to pay off
the mob!

CALVERT: I have your loan here, in coin.

> *He shows it.*

SIR JOHN: Your Shylock loan?! The price is too high!

CALVERT: I've offered the governor a loan, secured with –

SIR JOHN: – a terrible sacrifice!

JACK: Father! Inaction will cost us all our lives!

SIR JOHN: *(To CALVERT.)* They'll kill you too Calvert!

CALVERT: They know me, and I owe them nothing.

CONNIE: Sir John…

SIR JOHN: Connie?

CONNIE: Don't matter.

YORK: Sir! Do the deed! Think of me! My father will reward
your sacrifice.

SIR JOHN: He would, wouldn't he.

BARNARD: Come on man! What yer waiting for Hotham?!

SIR JOHN: Connie, my razor.

> *SIR JOHN quickly carries out the circumcision and delivers the foreskin to CALVERT. CALVERT hands over the coin. Enter, at pace, CAPTAIN MOYER with two soldiers. They secure the door behind them. The mob is still there. All three soldiers draw their swords.*

MOYER: Hold! Rest easy! Sir John Hotham! I am arresting you for treachery to Parliament!

JACK: What is the nature of this treachery?

MOYER: A conspiracy to surrender the town to the papists!

SIR JOHN: Captain Moyer, my dear chap, whatever are you talking about?

MOYER: You conspired with Lady Digby, Queen Henrietta's lady of the bedchamber to surrender Hull to the King's party.

YORK: *(Drawing his sword.)* Sirrah, I am the Duke of York, heir to the throne, and no papist, I know of no one at court called Lady Digby.

MOYER: *(Drawing sword.)* Yes, Lady Digby and Mademoiselle Frottage were inventions of mine and Sweet Lips designed to reveal Hotham's true intent, namely the betrayal of Parliament.

SIR JOHN: I am tricked! Undone.

> *RUPERT steps out of the curtains, and draws his sword.*

RUPERT: Ruprecht Pfalzgraf bei Rhein, Herzog von Bayern! The King's commander of horse!

YORK: Cuz! We are maligned, called papists!

RUPERT: Then the English Civil War starts now. Who will make the first advance?

A stand off. No one wishes to make the first move.

MOYER: Let it begin!

> *MOYER picks up the vase and deliberately smashes it on the floor. DRUDGE draws his knife and charges him with a blood curdling scream. Sword fight involving everyone. SIR JOHN takes his chance and escapes via the entrance that JACK had used to come in. The fighting freezes. CONNIE stands, holding two hat boxes, both looking rather heavy.*

CONNIE: My lord fled Hull on foot through the Beverley Gate, pursued by Captain Moyer and grapeshot.

> *SIR JOHN runs across the stage followed by MOYER with DRUDGE on his back beating him.*

I picked up the hat boxes, heavy for hat boxes, as their cargo was coin. The two thousand. Enough to buy into the bakers' guild. I wanted to call my baker's shop "Connie's" but the guild wouldn't allow a woman's name so I had to use my surname, alone, hence Greggs.

> *Enter SIR JOHN again. He meets a commoner on a horse, a wooden prop, or coconut shells.*

Sir John ran north where meeting a yeoman riding to Hull he declared himself to be the man's superior, and commandeered his horse.

SIR JOHN: I'm a baron, and a knight, and you're less than nothing, so hand over your horse. What's he called?

COMMONER: Radish.

SIR JOHN: *(Jumping on the horse.)* Come on Radish!

CONNIE: At Beverley he came upon a Parliament troop of cavalry. He took over command from their captain and ordered them to escort him to the family estate at Scorborough.

> *Enter SIR JOHN, slowly, with a troop of Parliament horse, SIR JOHN acting the part of commander.*

CONNIE: However, Captain Moyer had made good speed from Hull, and –

MOYER: *(Taking the bridle of HOTHAM's horse.)* Sir John Hotham, you are my prisoner! I arrest you in the name of the Commonwealth.

SIR JOHN: Since it must be so, I am content, and submit.

> *SIR JOHN kicks MOYER in the groin and runs off again, this time pursued by everyone.*

MOB: Wanker

CONNIE: Finally, he is cruelly beaten, secured and taken back to Hull, before being shipped to the Tower of London, and the scaffold where we began.

> *A tableau reprise of the prologue.*

CONNIE: *This man in his time played many parts,*
  Soldier, politician, baronet, lover
  Husband, father, loyalist, liar
  Turncoat, renegade, traitor

  Beheaded by the victorious Parliament party
  For his offer to the royals, the arsenal to bring
  Yet if the cavaliers had won the war
  He would have been executed by the King

  His place in Hull and history is secure
  And his own small act of revolution
  In denying the divine right of the monarch
  Began the English road to parliamentary constitution

> *The RANTER and COMPANY sing.*

JERUSALEM

THERE'S A PROMISE THAT IS WORTH THE YEARS OF TOIL,
AND IT NEEDS SOMEBODY TO BE THE PIONEERS.
IT'S A NOTION THAT WAS PLANTED IN OUR SOIL,
THAT WE'VE WATERED WITH OUR BLOOD AND SWEAT AND TEARS.
AND WE'D PLOUGH A THOUSAND FIELDS TO HELP IT FLOURISH
AND WE'LL HARROW AND WE'LL TILL UNTIL IT GROWS.
FOR TO NURTURE AND TO CULTIVATE TAKES COURAGE
IT'S FAR EASIER TO DENY THAN TO PROPOSE

WE WERE ANGERED
WE WERE LOOTED
WE WERE EASY TO CONDEMN
BUT WE'LL BE ANCHORED
WE'LL BE ROOTED
WHEN WE HAVE BUILT OUR JERUSALEM.

AND WE'D FACE A THOUSAND ARMIES TO PROTECT IT IN THE FIELD
OUR HONOUR AND OUR VOICES ARE OUR SHIELD.
OUR HOPE WILL BE A BEACON, A GUIDING LIGHT FOR ALL TO SEE.
NOW WE'VE SOMETHING TO BELIEVE IN, ENGLAND'S PROUD
DEMOCRACY

FOR WE WERE ANGERED
WE WERE LOOTED
WE WERE EASY TO CONDEMN
BUT WE'LL BE ANCHORED
WE'LL BE ROOTED
WHEN WE HAVE BUILT OUR JERUSALEM.

WE WERE ANGERED
WE WERE LOOTED
WE WERE EASY TO CONDEMN
BUT WE'LL BE ANCHORED
WE'LL BE ROOTED
WHEN WE HAVE BUILT OUR JERUSALEM.
WHEN WE HAVE BUILT OUR JERUSALEM.